Crossing
RIO
PECOS

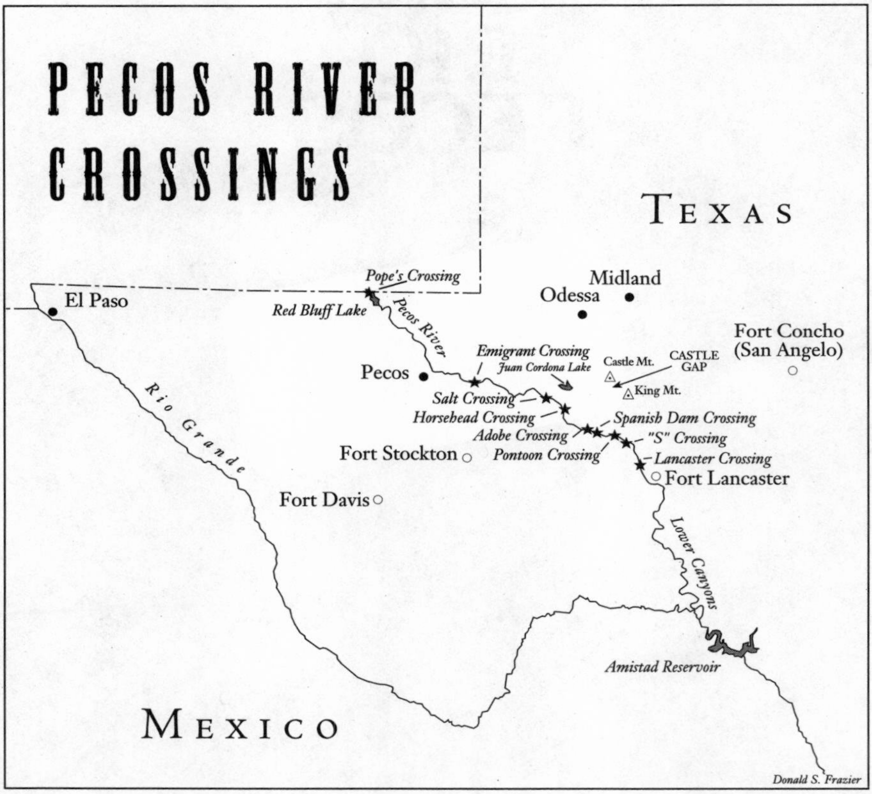

PECOS RIVER CROSSINGS

TEXAS

El Paso

Pope's Crossing

Red Bluff Lake

Pecos River

Midland

Odessa

Fort Concho
(San Angelo)

Pecos

Emigrant Crossing

Juan Cordona Lake

Castle Mt.

CASTLE
GAP

King Mt.

Salt Crossing

Horsehead Crossing

Spanish Dam Crossing

Adobe Crossing

"S" Crossing

Fort Stockton

Pontoon Crossing

Lancaster Crossing

Fort Lancaster

Fort Davis

Rio Grande

Lower Canyons

Amistad Reservoir

MEXICO

Donald S. Frazier

Crossing RIO PECOS

PATRICK DEAREN

Foreword by
Paul Patterson

CHISHOLM TRAIL SERIES • NUMBER SIXTEEN

TEXAS CHRISTIAN UNIVERSITY PRESS
FORT WORTH

Dearen, Patrick
    Crossing Rio Pecos / by Patrick Dearen.
        p.   cm.– (Chisholm Trail series ; no. 16)
    Includes bibliographical references and index.
    ISBN 0-87565-159-3 (pbk. ; alk. paper)
    1. Fords (Stream crossings) –Pecos River (N.M. and Tex.)–
    history. 2. Pecos River (N.M. and Tex.)–Description and
    travel. 3. Pecos River Valley (N.M. and Tex.)–History. I.
    Title. II. Series.
    F392.P3D43 1996
    976.4'9–dc20   95-26692
                                                            CIP

Design by Margie Adkins
Cover: Nineteenth century drawing of Horsehead Crossing in 1850
(originally published in John Russell Bartlett, *Personal Narrative of
Explorations and Incidents, Volume I*).

To my father, Delbert Dearen,
who introduced me early to the
headwaters of the Pecos.

★ Contents

A wagon crossing the Pecos, likely at Lancaster Crossing. (courtesy, Clayton Wheat Williams Collection, N. S. Haley Memorial Library, Midland, Texas)

I now love the old Pecos, but it has taken me seventy-five years. It has taken Pecos water-induced traumas that long to heal.

Patrick Dearen is well acquainted with that obnoxious, noxious, tortured, torturous stream of water going by the name of Pecos. Writer, photographer, backpacker, and tireless researcher, Dearen has been up and down the river countless times by canoe and on foot. Most of his labors have been afoot—plodding and trodding its Texas length, seeking out crossings. One could say that he has made deep tracks in and along Rio Pecos, deep to the point of being temporarily quicksanded on occasion.

Too, there is much work he has done inside—researching historical documents, old letters, maps, newspapers, and books, not to mention taped interviews with old-timers. Work, but not a chore, he says, taking into consideration the scores of nice people he has dealt with: librarians, museum curators, historians, newspaper people, old cowboys—in fact, everybody he has met along the way.

Down through the centuries, countless thousands of wayfaring strangers employed profane, obscene epithets against Rio Pecos as they crossed—and were double-crossed. Confide in any of them and they would concur with the following assessment:

> The devil could not dream such a damnable stream
> As the Pecos River Southwest;
> From bank to bank she reeked and stank
> Like a thousand buzzards' nests.

Back in the early 1920s, and for years thereafter, I hated the Pecos and did not hesitate to say so to its deceptively beautiful face. I repeated the terms especially while pack-jacking one-hundred-pound sacks of livestock feed up the treacherous bank of S Crossing when the wagonload proved too much for our work team, Babe and Nell.

Further back in time, I caught my first "goin'-swimmin'" truck from Rankin, Texas, down to the Pecos—seventeen miles. Here I learned that "last one in is a rotten egg." Indeed, rotten in more ways than one. The dirty, rotten straggler had drunk up and poured out our drinking water, leaving me at the mercy of that slimy, briny (though invitingly alluring) stream. I raced to the river, dropped down, and gulped swallow after swallow—until my taste buds had time to properly assay the stuff. The shock was paralyzing, and the purgative powers of that putrid Pecos potion were of such magnitude that the dose immediately sought through-passage.

Geologists apprise us of the fact that Rio Pecos water had wriggled and writhed some one million years passing through to the sea, yet it tarried only a millisecond or two passing through me. And I am not alone in this respect. I call to mind the fictional Sam McGoo family. They settled on the Pecos about the time the alkali did, hastily partook of a canteen of that water, and their stomachs haven't settled yet.

My final encounter with a Pecos River crossing was in 1931 at Girvin, Texas, trying to wishful-think five hundred head of spooky range horses into taking the crossing by bridge. If they wouldn't, we would be forced to trudge upriver and ford at Horsehead Crossing, which would thrill me today, but at that time, it meant just another twenty dreary miles out of the way. As it turned out, the most despised, rejected member of the herd—a lowly jackass—saved the day by leading the horses across the bridge.

In these pages, friends of libraries and addicts of the printed word will find Patrick Dearen and Rio Pecos a truly compatible couple. Or better said, perhaps, the former compatible and the latter combatable. But you will love them both. As I do.

Paul Patterson
Pecos, Texas
January 1995

The story of the Rio Pecos in frontier Texas is really the story of its crossings, for generally these vital "gateways to the west" harbored man's only intimate contact with a deadly river otherwise walled by barrier banks.

The crossings frequently flowed red with blood and echoed with the sounds of the mythic Old West—the war cry of the Indian, the blast of the cowboy's six-shooter, the crack of the stage driver's whip, the thunder of the stampeding longhorn. At the very time that documented history was painting dreary existences for pioneers in many other locations, the Pecos and its crossings stirred with color and drama and nurtured the stuff of legend. Indeed, the modern perception of the mythic Old West comes closer to fruition in the frontier Pecos country than virtually anywhere else.

Formed one-half to one million years ago,[1] the Pecos originates at 11,300 feet in the Sangre de Cristo range in northern New Mexico, a pristine stream splashing down through alpine forests and flower-spangled meadows. To the west of its headwaters, barely thirty air miles, flows the south-trending Rio Grande. Yet, the muddying Pecos sets a course to the southeast that will not see it intersect the Rio Grande for 926 sinuous miles.[2] At the point where the Pecos enters Texas, it splits a parched land 300 miles wide and thirsting in vain for a sister river.

Drawn by the life-giving Pecos waters, the so-called Clovis people may have camped on its banks and taken shelter in its lower canyon overhangs by 9000 B.C. These nomadic hunters, the first New World culture identifiable through archaeology, included or were close ancestors of Midland Man, whose eleven thousand-year-old remains surfaced in Midland County, Texas, fifty miles east of the

Pecos in 1953. By 8500 B.C., the Clovis culture had disappeared, and a new people, the Folsom, had emerged to leave their defining spear-point style in a mass buffalo kill in Mile Canyon near the mouth of the Pecos.

With the retreat of glaciers and the seasonal migration of buffalo to northern ranges by 7000 B.C., Folsom descendants chose to occupy the Pecos and live off the land. For the next 8,000 years, the lower canyon rockshelters nurtured these hunter-gatherers, who banded into family groups of up to thirty persons. Venturing through-out the Pecos country of Texas, these Indians hunted with the atlatl and spear, the bola (a thong with stones at either end), the curved rabbit stick, and, after its introduction in about A.D. 900, the bow and arrow.[3]

Late-prehistoric Indians of Texas, whether facing the river's lower canyons or upriver flats, coveted natural fords such as Salt Crossing near modern Imperial.[4] U.S. Army Brevet Captain John Pope, upon crossing the Pecos in March 1854, explained why:

> The river below the thirty-second parallel [the Texas-New Mexico line] changes its character from a rocky bed, with occasional rapids, to soft mud bottom and banks. Fording-places below this parallel are very rare, and present in all cases a depth of water which, at any other than the dry sea-son, absolutely prevents the passage of wagons or wheeled vehicles. . . . The banks are perpendicular, about ten feet high, and falling into the stream constantly—the deep water being uniform from one shore to the other.[5]

Even for buffalo, the epitome of strength and endurance, the Pecos was a barricade. In 1684, Spaniard Juan Dominguez de Mendoza and his party killed more than four thousand head east of the river but reported only a few bulls west of it.[6]

At the beginning of recorded history, the Pecos remained a magnet, luring Jumano Indians to its adjacent buffalo range and to nearby salt beds such as Juan Cordona Lake.[7] This fringe Puebloan culture, dominant along the Rio Grande from the Rio Conchos to near El Paso, was an odd blend of gardeners and nomads, either con-tent in their fields or restless for the chase. North and east of the Pecos, meanwhile, scattered bands of Tonkawas and Lipan Apaches trod a wilderness yet to see a modern horse.[8]

It was into such an empire, drained by a lone river, that the Spaniards pushed in the sixteenth century, driven by dreams of conquest, converts, and consummate wealth. Cabeza de Vaca came first, crossing this "great river coming from the north" in his epic 1535 trek from the Texas Gulf Coast to Sonora, Mexico.[9] In 1583, Antonio de Espejo followed the coils of the "Rio de las Vacas"—the River of Cows—or Pecos, from Cicuye pueblo near its headwaters to modern Texas. Probably at Salt Crossing, he met three Jumano hunters, who pointed his expedition and its horses and mules southwest to the Jumano settlements.[10] Seven years later, Gaspar Castano de Sosa, terming the Pecos the "Salado" or "Salt," struck it near its mouth and forged upstream to Cicuye.[11] Although Spaniards later would refer to the river as "Puerco"—pig-like or dirty[12]—by 1599 the name Pecos—a word of indeterminate origin—had come into use.[13]

Finding no precious minerals along the Texas stretch and few Indians willing to be proselytized, Spain retained little interest in the river. Soon, the Pecos and its desert gained a reputation that would endure until the late nineteenth century—as a forbidding land through which to hurry, not tarry.

With 7,000 horses, including breeding stock, introduced to the Southwest in 1598 by future New Mexico Governor Don Juan de Oñate, Indians gradually acquired the animals through straying, thievery, and trade. As early as 1659, Apaches north of the Pecos headwaters were a horse people, raiding New Mexican settlements, and within a few years the Comanches had become horse warriors without peer. In 1705, Comanches took to plundering Spanish settlements near the upper Pecos, and by the middle of the century, they had wrested the Southern Plains from the Apaches (who had absorbed the Jumanos into their culture) and driven the Lipans to the lower Pecos and Mexico. For the next 125 years, the Pecos River in Texas marked the southwestern boundary of Comancheria. Even the Comanches shunned its banks and elected instead to establish their rancherias far to the northeast and to push down each fall to cross at Horsehead Crossing and raid deep into Mexico.[14]

On into 1821, when Spain's dominion ended, and on through Texas's fifteen years as a province of Mexico and a near-decade as an independent nation,[15] the Pecos remained little known to white men. Snaking through a hostile wilderness far from settlements, it drew few pioneers other than *carreta* freighters, who claimed Juan Cordona Lake as the principal salt supply for northern

Mexico.[16]

The river's reputation as a gateway west began in 1849, four years after the United States admitted Texas to the Union and immediately after news of a California gold discovery filtered back east. Spawned by military and emigrant needs, three routes quickly opened up across the Pecos country—the Lower Road, which crossed at the Indian ford of Lancaster Crossing sixty-five air miles above the river's mouth; the Upper Road, which crossed another fifty-five miles upstream at Horsehead Crossing; and the Emigrant Road, which crossed at newly developed Emigrant Crossing, a little less than sixty miles below the New Mexico line. Within another decade, the U.S. Army opened a fourth ford, Pope's Crossing, immediately south of New Mexico, and this uppermost crossing quickly assumed much of the Upper Road traffic. Finally, in 1868, the U.S. Army rerouted the Upper Road to cross thirty miles below Horsehead and near a point that, with the laying of a bridge in 1870, became Pontoon Bridge or Crossing.

Horsehead, Lancaster, and Pope's ultimately gained renown above and beyond emigrant and military use. The Lower Road marked the route of the San Antonio-Santa Fe mail of 1851, the Texas-California Cattle Trail of the early 1850s, and the San Antonio-San Diego Mail of 1857. The Upper Road was even more famed, sharing its ruts with the Comanche war trail, the Butterfield Overland Mail of 1858-1861, and the Goodnight-Loving Cattle Trail of the mid-1860s. The Chihuahua Trail, a trade route between San Antonio and Chihuahua City, Mexico, touched or traced stretches of both roads, as well as the Jumanos' old trail to the Pecos.[17]

To guard the roads, the U. S. Army set up posts in the Pecos country: Fort Davis in 1854, ninety miles southwest of Horsehead Crossing;[18] Fort Lancaster in 1855, four to five miles east of Lancaster Crossing;[19] and Fort Stockton in 1859, thirty-four miles southwest of Horsehead.[20] But in 1861 Texas seceded, and the U. S. Army relinquished the region to the Confederacy.[21] The consequences to the Pecos were severe, not because of civil war but because the strife deprived the Texas frontier of a meaningful military presence for the next six years. Unchecked, Indians so terrorized the Pecos and eastern settlements that, by 1866, four of every five frontier ranches lay in ruins.[22]

At war's end, three million cattle grazed Texas ranges and could be purchased at $3 to $5 a head,[23] while markets to the north and northwest promised much greater prices. As other herds traced trails from the breeding grounds of Texas to the fattening ranges of the Great Plains, thousands of cattle forged up the Pecos corridor to New Mexico and beyond. By 1885, 5.7 million Texas beeves had made their way to other regions.[24]

Reestablishing on the Pecos in 1867,[25] the U.S. Army waged a final seven-year conflict with the Comanches, who stubbornly resisted reservation life. Meanwhile, buffalo outfits on the South Plains undertook their own war against the great herds on which the tribe was so dependent. The Comanches fell first, yielding their long dominion over the region to the army and its superior firepower in Palo Duro Canyon in the Texas Panhandle in 1874.[26] Nevertheless, the Indian threat was not over. Mescalero Apaches, with their hated enemies the Comanches gone, swooped down from their Guadalupe Mountains stronghold and New Mexico reservation to plague open-range ranches that sprang up along the Pecos in the 1870s.

The buffalo held on until 1879, when the last significant kill in Texas occurred at Mustang Springs, seventy miles northeast of the river that had long thwarted the animals' southwestward migration.[27] Ironically, on into the 1880s, the Pecos nurtured a small remnant herd that ranged close to Horsehead Crossing on the TX cattle outfit, which in 1879 took in forty miles of riverfront on either side.[28]

By early 1881, the Mescalero danger had ended. But the ranching tradition endured, eclipsing even a thriving farming industry that, with the first major diversion of Pecos water by 1877, had created Spanish Dam Crossing a dozen miles above Pontoon Crossing.[29]

As the Texas & Pacific Railroad, in 1881, and the Southern Pacific, in 1883, opened up the region to an entire continent, the Pecos was spawning a breed of cowboy unlike any other. F. S. Millard, who punched cattle on the Pecos in the 1880s, recalled a fellow cowhand saying that "he reckoned the Pecos boys were the most ex-pert cowboys in the world," and another responding, "Yes—with the *ex* left off."

The Pecos hands, said Millard, would "dash out, round up about 7 or 8 miles of the river, brand out, and go again [and] make about 4 roundups a day getting the cattle that were close to the water. But cattle went further from water in the Pecos country than any place I ever saw or heard of. There was big steers then, and they would go back 20 and, a few, 25 miles."[30]

"They'd water every other day. . . ," recalled Cliff Newland, who hired on with a Pecos country outfit about 1900. "I've been down there to that Pecos River [with the] morning clear, and in the foothills you could see the dust on the rise. That's when them old-time cattle would start in to get a drink of water, and the dust a-risin'. . . . There never was what you'd call a real fat cow or horse come off that Pecos River and drank that river."[31]

Cliff Newland in 1909. (courtesy,
Jack and Bonnell Newland)

With the currents depositing quicksand at many watering points, reliable cowboys paired up to "ride bog" for mired cattle, a task that may have led to the expression, "He'll do to ride the river with."[32]

"One of us would put a rope on them—around her horns so she wouldn't choke—and the other one would get down and tromp beside their legs. . . ," recalled Jim Witt, who took up cowboying around Emigrant Crossing in the 1920s. "There's a helluva suction in that ol' mud, and you break the suction that way—what you call `trompin' them out.' Sometimes you could just pull them out without trompin' them out, but if the ol' cow was kind of weak, well, you might have to tromp her out."[33]

Sometimes such efforts came too late.

"The Pecos was a graveyard for cattle, because of quicksand," remembered Barney Hubbs, who joined his father in homesteading a ranch fifty-five miles above Emigrant Crossing in 1908. "You'd water your cattle there, and at night they'd bog down in that river and then die, freeze to death. And then the next morning, why, you'd drag them out and skin them."[34]

Although such trials gave birth to the saying that cowboys feared only two things, rattlesnakes and the Pecos,[35] experienced hands saw an advantage in the river's crooks.

"Of a night, we would put our herd in a bend and [have] one man watch the gap at a time," said Millard. "It would not be over 30 feet wide and sometimes less, and I never knew of the cattle getting out . . . . Sometimes we would throw a small roundup in a bend and rope and brand our calves."[36]

But the Pecos offered pitfalls that were out of its cowboys' hands—lawlessness, cattle drift, and drought.

"There is said to be a great many outlaws congregated on the Pecos, from Lancaster up to the Seven Rivers [in New Mexico]," reported Texas Ranger Sergeant L. B. Caruthers in 1880. "A good many of them are between the New Mexico line and Horsehead Crossing and have been compelled to leave New Mexico. . . . They not only steal horses, etc. from the rancheros, but from the emigrants and freighters."[37]

The river's reputation as the "bad man's hell"[38] even gave rise to terms such as Pecos swap, meaning to steal,[39] and the verb *pecos*, meaning to murder a man and throw his body in a river such as the Pecos.[40]

In 1885 came the "Big Drift," when a seething mass of cattle, a hundred thousand strong, swept hellbent out of the far north-northeast with a blizzard nipping at their flanks. "It was impossible," said one cowboy who watched their passing, "to think of holding them back." As with the great buffalo herds before them, they never stopped until they reached the barrier Pecos. There they grazed the land bare and died by the thousands, even as wagon outfits from as far away as the Canadian River worked to return them to their home ranges. As late as 1902, a remnant of the Big Drift still tramped the Pecos banks.[41]

The unprecedented roundup of 1885 was over by July,[42] but by the end of August, drought had taken a devastating hold on the Pecos. It spread like a blight through the rest of Texas and on into eastern New Mexico, southern Arizona, and northern Mexico. "It never rained a drop from the fall of '85 till May '87," said Millard, who rode the Pecos throughout the lingering pestilence. By the spring of 1886, cattle again were dying on the river by the thousands, from a point in New Mexico 200 miles above the T&P Railroad to Lancaster Crossing a hundred miles below.

"The plains west of here are parched and dry, and the carcasses of thousands of cattle are to be seen in every direction . . . ," reported a Big Spring, Texas, correspondent on May 18. "Fully 20,000 carcasses cover the plains. The stench as one passes along the Texas Pacific west [toward the Pecos]. . . is terrible."

Inspecting a brief stretch of the Pecos in New Mexico that spring, one rider found 200 to 300 head of dead cattle bogged in the quicksands. Before the drought had broken, J. V. Stokes stood on the bank in Texas and watched forty cattle carcasses an hour float by. "Just imagine what a time we had," said cowhand W. C. Cochran, "working that country and drinking that water off those dead cattle in the spring of 1888."[43]

When the rains came, the ranch industry gained a reprieve that endured three decades before another drought crippled the river and the state. In the eighteen-month period between November 1, 1916, and May 1, 1918, the west-bank town of Pecos, eighteen miles above Emigrant Crossing, received a mere 2.90 inches of precipitation.[44] The plague was even more paralyzing east of the river, where Billy Rankin and his father ranched the Midland-Upton county line.

"In '16, '17, '18, altogether in the two years and eight months [of drought], it did not rain enough on that property to wet you one time in a light summer shirt," the younger Rankin remembered.[45]

The barren range forced some Pecos River ranchers to ship their cattle to holdings as far away as Arizona, while others could only sell or watch their beeves die.[46]

So unforgiving was this briny, treeless river that few pioneers ever referred to it in other than scathing terms. Consider the mood of young emigrant Hallie Stillwell in about 1902:

"We had been living on a ranch out in Pecos County and we were going to San Angelo to live. I had heard enough about the Pecos River, through the talk of the family, that I was dreading it. I was afraid, because I'd heard so many bad tales about people getting caught in the quicksand and having problems crossing. I just had an idea of going down and not being able to pull out of it. And so, [as] we approached it, I was in fear and trembling."[47]

Up and down the Pecos, throughout its Texas windings, such visceral emotion seemed to haunt its frontier crossings. ★

★ Chapter 2
Pope's Crossing

Guided by a lonely fist of rock, the lawless and the upright trailed to Pope's Crossing on the Pecos for three quarters of a century.

Down from present New Mexico the river came, a moat of brine and mud on a snake-track course bound for the creosote flats and wind-hewn sands of West Texas. Just below the border, it hesitated, as if unsure of the desert ahead. Hooking back to within a mile of New Mexico, it finally surrendered, turning southward to slither reluctantly through an unforgiving land.

Just downstream of that decisive bend and sunrise bluff, the riverbed hardened before a submerged outcrop of sandstone and limestone.[1] That outcrop may have borne up long-ago Indians afoot or on horseback as they crossed between a large camp on the west bank[2] and a hollow of fresh, cool water in a bouldered gulch on the east.[3] "There's a spring there," remembered early settler Clay Slack in 1968. "The water ran off of the rocks, and there was a pothole . . . [with] soft water."[4] Doubtless, early peoples coveted the spring, for it constituted the only source of good water on the east side of the Pecos for hundreds of miles.[5]

Equally rare along this canal of a river—with sharp, bare banks and vicious currents—were practicable crossings. The ruling Comanches, Kiowas, and Apaches of the mid-1800s apparently disdained even Pope's as a potential ford, for no such Indian crossing caught the attention of emigrant or U.S. Army parties skirting the site between 1849 and the mid-1850s. In March 1854, even its namesake, Brevet Captain John Pope, chose instead to cross upstream at the Pecos-Delaware confluence, two and one-third miles north of the New Mexico line.[6]

Born March 16, 1822, Pope graduated from West Point in 1842 and served in the Corps of Topographical Engineers in Florida and on the U.S.-Canada border. After duty in the Mexican War of 1846-1848, he served in Minnesota and, in 1851, became chief topographical engineer for the Department of New Mexico.[7] In his survey of the Pecos country along the thirty-second parallel in 1854, Pope found only a dearth of water shackling the route's promise as "the great and only highway across the Plains."[8] As a result, Congress appropriated $100,000, and the War Department dispatched Pope in quest of artesian wells along the Pecos in 1855.

Traveling overland with his command from port at Indianola, Texas, Pope halted on the east bank of the Pecos just above present Red Bluff Dam and constructed a fortified camp of adobe and native stone. "Pope's Camp," as it became known, served as headquarters and supply depot for the expedition, which, by means of mule power and steam engine, drilled three unsuccessful wells along the Texas-New Mexico line a few miles east of the Pecos.[9] During the three-year, disaster-plagued operation, Pope dispatched parties in all directions to map trails and detail the flora and fauna.[10] Scouting along the Pecos, his subordinates turned their horses into the water below the fist of rock and firmly established the crossing that would bear his name. His June 4, 1858, map pinpoints the unlabeled ford as situated three miles north-northwest of his "Main Camp" and one mile south of the New Mexico line.[11]

J. Evetts Haley, who first lodged in a cow camp one hundred yards east of the crossing at age eight in 1909, described it as a "wide-place in the river with sandy bottom and sloped [banks]. A big rock extended out there—the river came down and hit it, and looped right around it."[12] Added Clay Slack in 1968, "That was just a natural sand bar and crossing there."[13]

When Pope finally abandoned the drilling operation in the summer of 1858, leaving behind the corrosive waters that had bedeviled his machinery, he took time to reflect on the Pecos.

"I am almost sorry we are leaving here," he wrote from the banks of the river on August 21. "I have formed a sort of affection for this turbid, sinuous stream, on whose banks I have shivered and sweltered during the colds and heats of the last four years."[14]

His wildcatting expedition may have been "Pope's folly" to

New York newspapers of the day,[15] but it nevertheless opened up a crucial point of passage across the Pecos for emigrants and stages. From 1849 on, wagoners trekking west along the Upper Road had forded the Pecos at Horsehead Crossing and forged far upstream to the vicinity of the fist of rock before veering west for the Guadalupe Mountains and El Paso. Now the preferred course of action upon striking treacherous Horsehead was to turn upstream along the river's east bank and delay fording until Pope's Crossing.

It was just that route over which the first westbound Butterfield Overland Mail stage rumbled in September 1858. But stumps and scrub brush burdened "Pope's new road," recorded passenger Waterman Ormsby, who described the jolting of the stage as "almost interminable and insufferable." Wrote Ormsby:

"We . . . pursued our weary course along the edge of the plain, thumping and bumping at a rate which threatened not to leave a whole bone in my body. What with the dust and the sun pouring directly on our heads . . . I found that day's ride quite unpleasant."

Ormsby and stage driver Henry Skillman, both "inhaling constant clouds of dust and jolting along almost at snail's pace," reached Pope's Camp on the night of September 27. In bold relief against the western sky, the distant Guadalupe Mountains rose fortress-like. In front of the men, meanwhile, the moonlight played eerily along walls of the camp, now converted into a stage station. After downing a quick supper and acquiring a fresh four-mule team, they descended a gentle hill to the river flat and forded the waters of Pope's Crossing, which Ormsby described as "quite rapid and nearly covering the hubs of our wagon."[16]

For the next eleven months, Butterfield stages splashed across Pope's Crossing twice a week on their 2,795-mile, twenty-five-day blitzes between Tipton, Missouri, and San Francisco.[17] Then in August 1859, Butterfield officials—in consideration of the military presence at forts Stockton and Davis—ordered a route change that required stage drivers to cross Horsehead and push west to the two posts and through the Davis Mountains.[18]

With beef in demand at an Indian reservation at Fort Sumner, New Mexico, (far upstream from Pope's) in 1864,[19] dust clouds billowed as cattle herds moved north along the Pecos. As with the Butterfield route, Pope's Crossing proved crucial to the trail, which came to be known as the Goodnight-Loving, named for the two men whose 1866 drive fired the imaginations of cattlemen throughout Texas. Pooling their herds in the Brazos River country, thirty-year-old Charles Goodnight and fifty-four-year-old Oliver Loving of Weatherford bore south and west to the Pecos, striking it at Horsehead and pushing upstream on the east side.[20]

At Pope's Crossing, the cattle etched a trail down into the river and across, firmly establishing the site as the preferred crossing point on the Goodnight-Loving route. Although this forced the herd to recross (above present Carlsbad, New Mexico) in order to avoid Apache strongholds to the west, Goodnight's reasoning was sound. From Pope's Crossing to a location several days' travel upstream, he explained, the east side of the Pecos was "extremely undulating with sandhills which was very deep and loose, making it impractical for a trail."[21]

The succeeding miles to Fort Sumner held no special adventure, recalled Goodnight, because "the Comanches at that time had no knowledge of the drive and never occupied that part of the country, except occasional war parties to see that no one was there (to keep out other tribes). Therefore, we did not see an Indian on the entire trip."[22]

Loving would not always be so lucky. The following year, on his second drive with Goodnight, he paid with his life for daring the Pecos trail that would bear his name.

As their herd approached Pope's Crossing in late July 1867, U.S. Army headquarters for the District of Texas issued a warning to the commander at Fort Stockton, ninety-five miles southeast of the crossing: "It having been reported that *Indians are assembling at points*

A herd of 2,000 cattle at Pope's Crossing in 1910. (courtesy, J. Evetts Haley Collection, N. S. Haley Memorial Library, Midland, Texas)

on the Pecos River with view to raid on the settlements, you will keep your command . . . alert."[23] Unaware of the increased threat, Loving and Bill "One-Armed" Wilson parted with the herd and pushed on alone for Santa Fe, where government officials soon would give new contracts for beef. Fording Pope's, the two men lay up by day and rode by night for three days to avoid hostiles. Finally traveling in daylight on the fourth day out, the drovers fled the charge of a Comanche war party and made a desperate four-mile ride to the Pecos. Besieged on its bank, the pair fought off the Indians even as a bullet exploded through Loving's wrist and into his side. That night, believing his death imminent, Loving implored Wilson to escape and carry the news of Loving's fate to his family and Goodnight. As the moon sank toward the Guadalupe Mountains, Wilson parted with the blood-soaked man and crawled into the Pecos.

Incredibly, not only did Wilson survive—staggering on foot for three days back to the herd—but so, too, did Loving initially. Staving off Comanches through a second and third day, Loving finally slipped into the river and struggled six miles upstream to the next watering place. There, immobilized by hunger and loss of blood, he endured an additional three days before three Mexican wagoners and a boy rescued him. Carried to Fort Sumner, Loving underwent amputation yet succumbed to his wounds September 25.[24]

Too late to aid Loving and Wilson, Captain George Gamble and Fort Stockton's Ninth Cavalry scouted 350 miles up and down the Pecos from September 14 to October 3. They did not engage hostiles, but, upon reaching Pope's Crossing, Gamble noted the strategic importance of the ford, which he did not call by name: "The Pecos River is a crooked . . . stream, with a current of three miles an hour, its average depth about fifteen feet, and can be crossed by wagons [and] cavalry . . . near the mouth of the Delaware River. Average depth at the crossings about three feet."[25]

Floods, however, sometimes turned Pope's Crossing into a boiling mass that denied passage, as Maria Shrode and her emigrant party learned in 1870. Setting out from Sulphur Bluff, Texas, the second week in May, the wagon train intersected the Pecos at Horsehead Crossing on August 2 and fell in along the old Butterfield stage ruts that bore upstream.

The Pecos desert weather, always unpredictable, soon struck with fury, as Maria's diary reveals. On August 6 a shower laid the dust and cooled the air. Five days later, two heavy thunderstorms swamped the caravan, and a third rendered camp so boggy that the drovers could not herd the beeves, one of which fell to lightning. On the night of August 12, Maria lay wide-eyed, listening to the pounding of rain and the crack of thunder. Even upon reaching the abandoned walls of Pope's Camp the next evening, she and her fellows gained no respite. "Oh, what a rain fell on us last night," she wrote. "I have heard that it never rains here, but I tell you they have some very heavy dews."

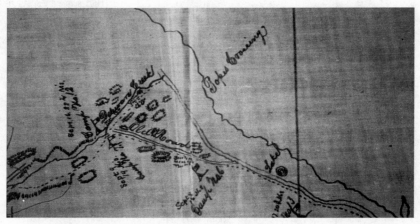

Captain S. T. Norvell's field map of his September 1875 scout to the vicinity of Pope's Crossing. (National Archives)

Relinquishing the lead the next morning to a cattle herd headed up the Goodnight-Loving Trail, the Shrode party soon proceeded to Pope's Crossing only to find the Pecos on a rampage born of runoff. "Came to the river and could not cross," wrote Maria. "The river was too high and rising. I went to a bluff and found some pure rain water in some holes in the rocks and got a bucket full of good water."

The emigrants continued their vigil throughout the next day, and the one after that, only to find the river still rising fast. Finally, on the third day, they yielded to the crossing's sovereignty and continued upstream along the east bank. It was not until they had journeyed to within ten miles of modern-day Roswell, New Mexico, that they managed to ford, twenty full days after Pope's Crossing first had turned them away.[26]

The Indian threat on the Pecos intensified in the 1870s,

generating more U.S. Army scouts to Pope's. In 1873, George Owens of the Twenty-fourth Infantry marched with Colonel Ranald Mackenzie eastward to the Pecos, striking it near Fort Lancaster and crossing at Horsehead. Bearing west, they encountered Indians on Carriso Flat between Fort Davis and El Paso, then scouted through the Quitman Mountains and back to the Pecos at Pope's. There, Owens and Mackenzie found cattle grazing the open range, and, at old Pope's Camp, a few settlers and a store.[27]

Spurred by the report of a cattle herd taken by Indians, Captain F. S. Dodge and Company D of Fort Stockton's Ninth Cavalry scouted up and down the Pecos between the Great Falls and Pope's Crossing from September 3 to September 12 of that year. Fording to Pope's east bank and camping September 9, Dodge found no recent Indian signs at this locale, which he termed "very barren."[28]

Three weeks later, on October 4, an officer and fifteen men of Company D, Ninth Cavalry, marched from Fort Stockton to Pope's Crossing after ranchers sighted Indians on the Pecos. Despite scouting for twelve days and 255 miles, they also failed to engage their enemies.[29]

With Mackenzie's defeat of Comanches and Kiowas in the Texas Panhandle in 1874,[30] the threat on the Pecos from those tribes ended. Nevertheless, hostile Apaches continued to prowl Pope's Crossing and to prey on ranchers such as John Chisum, who ran cattle along the Pecos in southern New Mexico.

"I don't think Chisum could be beat as a cowman, but he seemed to want the Pecos River to himself," recalled cattleman James P. Jones. "The Indians did not get so very many of his cattle, but they gave his horses thunder. There were two years that they kept him afoot and he never branded a calf."

At Seven Rivers, New Mexico, in 1875, Jones also suffered saddle stock losses to Apaches. Discovering the theft of fifteen animals, Jones and his brother, John, took up the trail in the company of Marion Turner and John Powell. A day and night behind the marauders, they tracked them far downstream to Horsehead Crossing and to a ranch below, where they learned that the Indians had taken an additional one hundred horses and hooked back to the north. Determined, the Jones party stayed on their trail, even as it carried them into the dry and forbidding sandhills.

"[The Apaches] got water by scratching down in the sand,"

James P. Jones recalled fifty-two years later. "We did not know that, and when our canteens ran out, we ran out of water . . . . We carried no pack outfit, but tied a little stuff on our saddles and nearly starved to death."

From the sandhills, the trail took the men west to Pope's Crossing and sixty more miles to Guadalupe Peak, before they finally gave up the chase.[31]

Travel along the Pecos proved especially perilous in early September 1876, when twenty-two-year-old A. M. "Gus" Gildea and Thomas W. Swilling headed out for Arizona from Menard County, Texas. Twenty-five miles west of Fort Concho (at present San Angelo), they met a cavalry detachment and telegraph line repairman who warned of an ensuing country "lousy" with Indians and impassable without escort. Undaunted, they rode on to the isolated Centralia stage station, where the sergeant in command also advised that they turn back. Still they rode, nooning where Apaches had camped the previous night and crossing a north-south Indian trail (only five hours old) near Castle Gap. Hoping to hit Horsehead Crossing under the cover of darkness, they pushed on far into the night, only to yield to exhaustion and to bivouac two hundred yards off the trail. They reached Horsehead about nine o'clock the next morning, only hours behind two war parties, and turned upstream for distant Pope's Crossing.

Finally reaching Pope's, Gildea and Swilling watered their horses and filled canteens before retreating behind a butte a half-mile away to camp. Daybreak brought a fine mist, leading the men to roll their weapons in their bedrolls before building a fire. Suddenly, Apaches were upon them, firing a single shot from the butte before fleeing toward the Pecos. Gildea seized his weapon and, from 150 yards, fired four quick shots that killed an Indian, wounded a second, and felled a horse. He watched them change their course for the south and then east, where, on another butte three-quarters of a mile away, they buried their dead comrade. The next day, so a cowhand told Gildea, the war party forded the Pecos, presumably at Pope's Crossing.

Crossing at the site themselves shortly afterward, Gildea and Swilling soon found work punching cattle for John Chisum in southern New Mexico. In the bitter cold of November, as they pushed an Arizona-bound herd to the fringe of the Mescalero Apache Reservation in New Mexico's Sacramento Mountains, the two men and their nineteen fellow drovers braced for a confrontation. At day-break, the Mescalero Apache chief, Solomon, and twenty warriors approached but withdrew without hostilities erupting. As the herd proceeded to the reservation, Gildea and a second cowhand went ahead to discourage the Indians from stampeding the beeves. While the reservation agent conferred with Solomon and cleared the way, Gildea met up with the Indian he had wounded at Pope's Crossing.

"He was convalescing, but as poor as a snake, my bullet having struck him in the back, passing through the right nipple," Gildea recalled decades later. "I told him I shot him and killed one and a horse. Several stood by him who said they were there and all seemed pleased to see me and shook hands and asked for el otro? (the other man). I told them he was with the herd and they said bueno, and rode to meet the herd."[32]

A final flurry of Indian depredations in the region in 1879 spurred the U.S. Army into the field along the Pecos. On April 7, Colonel George A. Armes embarked from Fort Stockton with fifty enlisted men, a second lieutenant, a surgeon, sixty horses, and fifteen pack mules. In a five-month campaign, his command chased the ghosts of Apaches to Pope's Crossing several times.[33] Armes himself crossed at the site on the fourteenth of May—a month in which detachments of his company marched 1,426 miles without engaging in any hostilities greater than felling forty rabbits on the Pecos near the crossing.[34] Three and a half months later, on September 3, Second Lieutenant John Bigelow, Jr., likewise made a fruitless scout to the ford.[35]

But even as the Apache danger faded into the past, outlaw violence already was threatening at Pope's and down the Pecos. "The people are always on the lookout for the outlaws from Mexico and the Pecos," reported Texas Ranger L. B. Caruthers on June 8, 1880.[36]

The river gained its reputation as a badman's den at the close of the Civil War, and by the time the Robert Casey family emigrated from Central Texas to New Mexico in the winter of 1866-1867, it was not uncommon to find gruesome evidence of "the uncertainty of life" on its lawless banks. "We stayed at the [Horsehead] crossing about three days. . . ," recalled Casey's daughter Lily Klasner, who was five at the time. "At the river he [Casey] found a body in shallow water. . . . The man had been stabbed five times. A piece of rope had been tied to the body for dragging it to the water's edge. On the bank there was no sign, and Father concluded that the corpse might have floated down the river, possibly for a long distance. He and the Mexicans dug a shallow grave, wrapped the body in a piece of canvas, and buried it."[37]

The situation did not improve even when the U.S. Army reoccupied Fort Stockton in 1867. In mid-August 1868, for example, twelve heavily armed Mexican riders, supposedly in quest of Indians, passed through Fort Stockton en route to the Pecos, thirty-four miles northeast. Citizens and military authorities soon came to know them as perpetrators of a "Pecos swap."

"They are a dangerous party and undoubtedly have been hanging around for the purpose of stealing stock," reported Captain Gamble, commander of Fort Stockton. "Citizens have reported to one having seen them painted [with war paint]."

At Horsehead Crossing, the Mexicans made their swap— trading violence for four horses from cattle drovers bound for El Paso. Captain Gamble and his command captured nine of the outlaws in late August, but the other three escaped toward Mexico with the stolen horses.[38]

In November 1872, a man named Little fell victim to "pecosing" shortly after fording Pope's Crossing in a two-horse wagon and setting up camp near Pope's Camp. Headed back down the Goodnight-Loving Trail with five or six cowboys who had helped him drive a herd north, Little reportedly guarded $24,000 in gold coins he had acquired in the sale of the beeves. Fearing a conspiracy, Little wandered from camp that night and possibly hid the money. His fears were well founded, for upon his return a cowboy murdered him for the bonanza.

In South Texas the following January, self-described cattle thief W. S. Wheeland met a member of the Little party named Ike Sneed. "He told me a man named R____ killed Little but only about eighty dollars was found . . . ," recalled Wheeland in 1892. "Sneed seemed to regret the loss of the money. . . . In 1886 I was in Topeka, Kansas, and met another of the Little party. He also told me R____ was at the head of the plot and that only seventy or eighty dollars were found with Little, and he believed the [remaining] money was hid about Pope's old camp."[39]

One of the bloodiest pecosings occurred in December 1872, only one month after the murder of Little. Riding down the Pecos on the fourteenth after pushing a cattle herd up the Goodnight-Loving Trail, Ed Gregory and his party came upon a deserted camp of five or six wagons about eight miles upstream of Horsehead Crossing. Studying the scene, they made a grisly discovery—the mutilated body of Peter Turner of Fort Concho.

"The murder was committed . . . with an axe by means of which his head was nearly severed from the body," Gregory reported to Fort Stockton's commander.

Papers and other signs at the camp indicated that Turner and four or five Mexican teamsters had been en route up the Pecos to obtain salt from Juan Cordona Lake in present Crane County.

"It appears . . ," wrote Gregory, "that he was murdered by his own men, in part for the money he is supposed to have had with him, but more particularly for his horses and arms. . . It is quite evident his murderers at once set out traveling in direction of. . . [Fort Stockton], probably with the intention of entering Mexico at del Norte [present Ojinaga]. . . . The trail showed they had four horses and was seen passing up near the Agua Bonita. . . . The murder was so foul and brutal that every effort should be used to secure the criminals."[40]

According to correspondence between Forts Concho and Stockton on December 30, parties returning to Fort Concho from the Pecos had encountered the gang at Horsehead Crossing shortly after the murder.[41] Believing the outlaws to be Mexico-bent, Second Lieutenant John Conline and his Fort Stockton command pursued the trail southwest.

"I proceeded to Presidio del Norte, Mexico, and by rapid marches endeavored to overtake the murderers . . . ," he reported on January 5, 1873. "Failing in this, I communicated my objective to the custom house officers on the American side of the Rio Grande opposite village Ojinaga, Mexico, and then crossed the river."

Despite Conline's raid into Mexico, the outlaws escaped.[42]

Post-mortem evidence of another murder along the Pecos—presumably at Pope's Crossing—surfaced in the early 1870s when A. D. Cantrell helped punch a cattle herd up the Goodnight-Loving Trail for R. K. Wylie and Sam Coggin. "Just after we crossed the Pecos," Cantrell recalled more than a half-century later, "one of our men, named Jordan, found a man's boot sticking out of the ground and called me. I took hold of the boot, heel and toe, and off it came with the foot in it."

Realizing they had found a shallow grave, the drovers decided to exhume the body to learn the person's identity and manner of death.

"It was not covered more than eighteen inches deep . . . ,"
remembered Cantrell. "Decomposition had begun and we could not
tell anything about it. He had on a good gray suit, but there was
nothing in his pocketbook, excepting three coppers and a half dozen
bullets; so we put it down that he had been robbed and murdered
instead of being an Indian victim, as we had supposed. I took the bullets, for in those days one could never have too much ammunition .
. . . We buried the body as best we could."[43]

It would not be the last lonely grave lying all but forgotten
at Pope's Crossing.

"Just around the bend on the river there, why, there's three
graves . . . ," Clay Slack noted in 1968. "I believe two of them are
emigrants that died a natural death. But one of them was a cowpuncher that was killed by Bob Olinger over a poker game or something."[44]

Olinger, described by New Mexico territorial Governor Lew
Wallace as "amongst the most bloody of the 'Bandits of the Pecos,'"
was born circa 1841 in Ohio and drifted to the Pecos country about
1876. Dubbing himself "Pecos Bob," he soon gained a bad reputation
stemming from his nasty disposition and imposing appearance. "He
was just a big, roughneck, over-bearing fellow," recalled acquaintance Charles Ballard. Six feet tall and weighing 240 pounds,
Olinger had a "gorilla-like chest that bulged out so far his chin
seemed to be set back in his chest," remembered Bell Hudson, anoth-

Bob Olinger. (courtesy, Robert N. Mullin Collection,
N. S. Haley Memorial Library, Midland, Texas)

er acquaintance. "He had a heavy bull neck, low-browed head, short and wide, topped with shaggy hair, bushy eyebrows, and a hat-rack mustache. His arms were long and muscular, with fists like hams. Despite his build and size he was quick as a cat . . . . He loved to show off, and it was one of his tricks to throw his .45s and keep a string of fire from both muzzles as long as the bullets lasted."

All too often, the gunfire was for more than show. Olinger's later superior, Sheriff Pat Garrett, styled him his "killer deputy," while acquaintance Gus Gildea branded him a "damned rascal" who "deserved killing."

Walking both sides of the law, Olinger served as town marshal at Seven Rivers before rumors that he abetted outlaws led him to withdraw to the Pecos and a cattle ranch he operated with his brother. "They had about 1,500 cattle when I was there," recalled W. Wier. "The ranch was on . . . [the east] of the Pecos, from the Arrow Camp [in New Mexico] down to Pope's Crossing."

On the ford's east side, at a rock house dating to the late 1870s, W. R. "Jake" Owen witnessed the killing spoken of by Slack. "I saw that—as cold-blooded a murder as was ever committed on God's green footstool . . . ," said Owen in 1937.

> There was [H. J.] Raymond and this fellow there in that camp. . . . [Andy Boyle and] I come up there with Bob Olinger. . . . They got down off their horses . . . and I stayed a little behind. I got down off of mine and tied it and started to the house. . . . [Olinger] walked right up to this fellow and shook hands with him, and then grabbed his right hand with his left and pulled out his pistol and shot him. Never a word passed. I wasn't more than ten steps from him. . . . I never did know what it was about, and Andy Boyle never did know. He [Olinger] didn't say anything to us, not as to what the killing was about. . . . We always just thought that he [the victim] was stealing horses, but whether he was or not, I don't know. . . . We buried him across a little canyon right west of the rock house.

Despite the murder and Olinger's clear involvement in other slayings, authorities pinned a U.S. deputy marshal's badge on him in 1880 and sent him riding with Pat Garrett in a November raid of outlaw hangouts along the Pecos in New Mexico.

Prone to bullying and taunting, Olinger finally met his match when authorities charged him with guarding captured killer Billy the Kid in the Lincoln County (New Mexico) Courthouse in April 1881. Confrontation brewed from the beginning, for the two men hated one another and made no attempt to disguise it. On April 28, the Kid made his break, killing Deputy James W. Bell with a pistol and ripping apart Olinger's face and chest with thirty-six fatal buckshot from Olinger's own shotgun.[45]

Outlaws such as Olinger haunted not only Pope's Crossing but also a bypassed river channel known as Rock Corrals a short distance downstream. Funneling stolen cattle up and down the Pecos and across Pope's, thieves needed only to seal the ends of the gorge with brush to form a natural holding pen for the beeves.[46] Infamous for violence and pecosings, Rock Corrals held another noteworthy danger—rattlesnakes, as L. B. "Bill" Eddins learned while cowboying on the encompassing Sid Kyle Ranch for seven years beginning in 1918. One November Eddins and another cowboy were building a fence across the rift, which is now hidden by Red Bluff Lake.

"It's kind of a rock canyon that runs down through there," Eddins recalled seven decades later. "It was about as deep as the ceiling, I guess. It's short, but it starts right there at the fort [Pope's Camp] and drops off. It wasn't straight-off, but it run down and [had] a ledge of rocks there, and there'd be hollow places back under it."

Busy erecting fence at the gully's brink, Eddins paid little attention to the other ranch hand's query about rattlesnakes as the second man prepared to drop off the far rim.

"I didn't even look, but I said, `Naw, I didn't see any rattlesnakes.' He stepped off that ledge and one rattled under him and he stepped over three before he got to the bottom."[47]

While rattlesnakes and outlaws denned in Rock Corrals in the 1870s, gunman Bill "Barney" Gallagher prowled Pope's Crossing and preyed on passersby from his Pecos River camp a short distance above the ford. Called a "robber of the west" by a contemporary Austin, Texas, newspaper, Gallagher, also called "Buckshot," had ties to Carrizo Springs in Dimmit County, where he may have punched cattle. During the months immediately preceding September 1876, authorities at Fort Clark, Texas, tried Gallagher for the killing of a U. S. soldier. Acquitted, he drifted to the Pecos, where he and a partner named Boyd pursued criminal ways.

At a cow camp on John Chisum's South Springs Ranch on

September 22, 1876, Gallagher and Boyd confronted four cowhands, including thirty-four-year-old John Slaughter and a man named Tobin. Despite the sawed-off shotgun in Gallagher's hands, Slaughter rode toward him, jerked out a pistol, and fired several quick shots. As Boyd spurred his horse into flight, Gallagher fell forward from the saddle, his breast and thigh spewing blood. Taken to a nearby store, he clung to life for ten hours while he confessed his evil deeds and prayed fervently. "He was game when fighting," the *Austin Democratic Statesman* of October 17 reported, "but a very coward when at last death came."[48]

In a bizarre footnote to the Gallagher saga, Lon Neil of Dallas and Philip Rock of Columbus, Texas, died in a fight over Gallagher's revolver and silver-mounted hat. Rock already was well known to San Antonio law officers, who were not sorry to see him ride out of town in the dust of a Slaughter cattle herd in 1876. Along the Pecos, Rock and Neil—both branded "dangerous men" by a newspaper of the day—met up with Gallagher. The latter gunman supposedly willed his six-shooter and hat to either Rock or Neil. In the Silverstein Saloon at Fort Stockton twenty-five days after his death, the dispute over ownership exploded into violence.

Evidently to agitate Neil, Rock invited several black soldiers to join them for a drink. Neil snapped that he did not drink with Negroes, then drew his weapon and began pistol-whipping the soldiers. Rock, apparently expecting Neil to assault him as well, whipped out his own pistol as a precaution.

Neil saw the firearm in his rival's hand and immediately shoved the muzzle of his own pistol into Rock's breast. After they exchanged words, bullets from the two men's pistols exploded into one another's torso.

Neil fell, and Rock staggered toward him, crying, "I'm shot in the bowels and will die, so I will give you some more from principle!" Taking aim, he emptied his six-shooter into Neil's skull, killing him.

When Rock died five hours later, townspeople buried the two men just as they had perished—Neil with boots on, Rock with boots off, face-to-face in the same grave.[49]

Pecos badmen were especially troublesome in and near the community of Fort Davis, as Texas Ranger Caruthers noted on June 14, 1880, in correspondence to Adjutant General J. B. Jones. "This is the rout[e]," he wrote, "that the thieves are compelled to travel from their haunts on the Pecos some one hundred twenty-five miles northwest of this point, to the Rio Grande, some ninety miles south."[50]

In requesting help from Governor O. M. Roberts on May 21, 1880, Presidio County Attorney John M. Dean of Fort Davis noted that "Many lawless men congregate around the cattle camps in New Mexico and from there they come in large parties to depredate upon the peaceable and law abiding citizens of this state. . . . During the past twelve months numerous murders and robberies have been committed in this county by their armed bands of desperadoes. . . .

"They usually operate in the following manner. On entering a store they present their guns and pistols and order everyone to hold up their hands and then one of the robbers ransacks the premises and reaches the persons of the proprietors."[51]

From June 1, 1879, to June 1, 1880, the crimes in Fort Davis and the encompassing county of Presidio included nine armed robberies during which one man was murdered and two others assaulted; an additional murder; the burglaries of four homes and one store; and saddle stock thefts either by outlaws or Indians.

Authorities captured suspects in only six of the cases, with the outlaws breaking jail on three occasions and two of the escaped parties eluding recapture. In a fourth jailbreak, outside gang members murdered one jailer and severely beat a second in springing three outlaws.[52]

One of the most daring armed robberies came in May 1880 when Jesse Evans and two of his twenty gang members struck a Fort Davis store in broad daylight. A short time earlier, the twenty-seven-year-old ally—and foe—of Billy the Kid had driven a cattle herd from New Mexico to Fort Stockton, presumably by way of Pope's Crossing. Disposing of the herd, the Evans gang pushed on to Fort Davis, where, about 5:00 p.m. on May 19, Evans, Albert "Bud" Graham, and Charles Groves Graham brazenly entered the Sender and Seibenborn store. Brandishing firearms and ordering hands raised, they seized $1,130 in money, watches, and merchandise.

Ranger Caruthers, reporting twenty-six days later from Fort Davis, spoke of the "absolute fear" that the threat of such crimes evoked in citizens, even with the timely capture of Bud Graham in Fort Stockton and the reported flight of Evans and Charles Graham to Horsehead Crossing. "The merchants here expect to be attacked daily. . . ," wrote Caruthers. "The outlaws are lying out in the mountains, in gangs of five to seven, watching this point and Stockton."

Evans's known association with the Pecos ended July 3, 1880, when Texas Rangers captured him in a gun battle in Pinto Canyon southwest of present-day Marfa. Convicted of second-degree murder, robbery, and assault, Evans entered the state penitentiary at Huntsville on December 1. A year and a half later he escaped to disappear mysteriously into history.[53]

The best-known shootist enmeshed with Pope's Crossing was Clay Allison, whose gravestone in the city of Pecos, Texas, bears the epitaph "He never killed a man who did not need killing." Born in 1840, Allison sent several men to early graves in the Southwest, yet he never lost his reputation as a gentleman.

Clay Allison. (courtesy, West of the Pecos Museum, Pecos, Texas.)

"He was a good-hearted man," recalled rancher George Coe, who knew Allison in Colfax County, New Mexico, where some of Allison's most violent episodes occurred.

In the early 1880s, Allison laid aside his guns, acquired the M. L. Pierce cattle outfit at Pope's Crossing, and became a peaceable

The old Clay Allison headquarters at Pope's Crossing in about 1910. (courtesy, J. Evetts Haley Collection, N. S. Haley Memorial Library, Midland, Texas)

and respected rancher. With a spring 200 yards above the ford offering ample drinking water, Allison set up headquarters in the line-camp house where Bob Olinger had killed a man so callously.

"I worked for him [Allison] there in 1880 and . . . [for] about three years," recalled W. R. Owen, who had helped lay the rock for the house a hundred yards from the crossing. "He was easy to get along with."

Styling his spread the P Ranch, Allison branded 700 to 2,000 head of cattle with two Ps on the left side and ran them on the open range.

"There never was any crowding of the range by new men and no trouble over range rights," recalled A. T. Windham, who rode line in the Pope's vicinity for the Seven Rivers Cattle Company after its founding in 1883. "He made no objection to the Seven Rivers company coming in."

Another Pecos cowhand, B. A. Oden, recalled Allison's infirmities during the gunman's latter ranching days. "He was too crippled to ride," said Oden, "therefore I did not see much of him, but I stayed with him one night in '86."

To obtain supplies, Allison would ford Pope's Crossing by wagon and travel forty-five miles downstream along the west bank to Pecos City (now Pecos), where he eventually took up residence and came to know R. D. Gage. Gage, who eventually married Allison's widow, recalled in 1929:

> I knew Mr. Allison very, very well. . . . He was a tall man, possibly six feet one inch in height, slender waisted, but broad shouldered, with black hair, piercing black eyes, making altogether quite a fine figure of a man. He had a habit of dress which was somewhat peculiar for that period and sec-

tion of country. When he would return home from his trips to the ranch, he would don a white shirt and would array himself in a well-fitting suit of black broadcloth.

Although Gage noted that Allison possessed "many very excellent and sterling qualities" and that the relationship between the two men was always "amicable," he could not forget the gunman's darker side.

He was a dangerous man to cross, especially if he were intoxicated. . . . He was never boisterous in his cups, but on the contrary, when drinking, the devil lights would dance in his eyes and his voice would drop to almost a whispering tone. If he liked you he was a strong friend, but toward them with whom he had a difference he was a dangerous enemy.

Ironic for a person who, as Gage said, "had the reputation of having killed two or three men," Allison died not in a gunfight but in a wagon accident. En route to Pope's Crossing from Pecos City in his heavily laden wagon in 1887, he mysteriously pitched to the ground, where a surging wheel crushed his skull.[54]

With the passing of Clay Allison, the east-side range land bordering Pope's Crossing fell into the hands of John Camp[55] and, in the early 1900s, John A. Haley. Dubbing his spread the 69 Ranch, Haley added a room to the old Allison camp and made it his headquarters.[56]

Clay Allison's grave and foot stone in Pecos, Texas. (author)

His son, J. Evetts Haley, had the privilege of witnessing one of the last major cattle drives to Pope's Crossing and beyond. "We were living in Midland and we'd go up there," he recalled more than eight decades later. "There was a big herd came by—watered there at least, didn't cross. . . . About two thousand head going up the old Goodnight Trail in 1910."[57]

Fences soon closed the remnant trail, but through the 1920s a few small herds still crossed Pope's from east to west to reach shipping points on the railroad stretching between the towns of Pecos and Carlsbad, New Mexico. Recalled Norman Eisenwine:

> In August of 1927 I was just seventeen years old. I was working for a rancher named Howard C. Collier, and he had a lot of land up there around Angeles and up the river. Angeles is where we was headed that day—they used to have a stock pen there. It's on the west side, and we had been working cattle on the east side. So I and a cowboy named Levi London drove about thirty-five saddle horses across the river at Pope's Crossing, and then come back down to Angeles to start working there. . . . The horses had no trouble crossing [the ford] at all. It wasn't boggy, and there was kind of a low bank on each side, I'd say for probably fifty yards, kind of sandy. There was cedars and greasewood, not much grass—

Norman Eisenwine in 1993. (author)

it'd been tromped out. The water was about up to my horse's stomach in the deepest part, and about thirty yards wide. That's the only time I was ever there.[58]

The end of an era came in 1936, when laborers completed Red Bluff Dam on the Pecos just downstream from Pope's Camp. [59] During the succeeding months, the briny waters inundated the lonely outpost, the old Clay Allison cow camp, the fist of rock—and Pope's Crossing. Now long-lost, the ford whispers not a hint of its vital role in opening the frontier. ★

Red Bluff Lake in 1995 at the site of Pope's Crossing. (author)

The waters and northeast bank of Emigrant Crossing as seen today. (author)

★ Chapter 3
Emigrant Crossing

It once flowed red with the blood of eighteen people massacred near its banks.

Emigrant Crossing, splitting the Pecos River twelve miles southeast of present Barstow, long stood as both a threat and a doorway for wagoners trekking west along the Emigrant Road to California. The discovery of gold near Sutter's Mill in California in January 1848 set in motion this human stampede,[1] intent not only on gold, but also on land ready for the taking in the West. The hopes of a big strike dwindled over the years, but the quest for land grew only stronger, bringing wagons creaking west along the trail to Emigrant Crossing as late as 1908.[2]

Opened in 1849, the Emigrant Road struck out from Fort Smith, Arkansas, and crossed the Red River into North Texas at Preston, south of Fort Washita. Bearing southwestward, it skirted Comanche and Kiowa water holes at present-day Big Spring and Mustang Springs, slashed through a sea of drifting sand, and, almost five hundred miles from Fort Washita, intersected the Pecos at Emigrant Crossing. Once across, emigrants either headed upstream to the Delaware River and pushed west through Guadalupe Pass or turned downstream and veered south and west for Monument Springs and the Davis Mountains.[3]

Among the intrepid forty-niners who challenged the Emigrant Road were the 101 men, nine women, and twenty-five children in the Strentzel wagon train that headed west from the Dallas vicinity in the spring of 1849. Louisiana Strentzel, in a

December 10, 1849, letter to her parents in Fannin County, Texas, spoke of the "hardships and privations" and "dangers and difficulties" with which the "wilderness of eighteen hundred miles" besieged them.

"We had not even a guide to direct us the way," recalled her husband, John Theophil Strentzel, forty-one years later. "Nothing except a map and compass to go by. The country was entirely unknown to us, not one of the party even having been through it."

No stretch of the road beleaguered the Strentzel group more than the plains and sand between modern-day Big Spring and Emigrant Crossing in late May.

Seventy miles and three days of arid wasteland sapped water barrels and exhausted the teams. One man died of liver disease, and physician Strentzel held little hope for his wife, who suffered from diarrhea, severe fever, and fatigue. "Having only one quart of water left, I would give to her and the two little children each a spoonful at a time to moisten their throats," he related. "Late in the afternoon our teams became so exhausted that they began to reel and stagger, seeming ready to drop down, and we had almost given up in despair, [when] the water hunters . . . came riding up, waving their hats and shouting, 'Water! Water! Water!'"

In the sandhills, the advance riders had stumbled upon pure, cold pools.

The argonauts camped there a week, recuperating, readying for the push on toward the Pecos. Still, by the time they reached Emigrant Crossing, the bodies of five more persons lay in lonely graves along the trail behind.

Finding the Puerco, or Pecos, "a narrow, deep, muddy stream," wrote Louisiana, the party constructed boats from wagon beds and ferried across on June 3, pulling the wagons across with ropes and swimming the animals. Two miles upstream the next day, the wagon tires fell into the three-day-old tracks of an eight-family, one-hundred-man wagon train party heading west from San Antonio.[4]

Even the U.S. Army relied heavily on the trail-blazing exploits of argonauts such as the Strentzels. Captain Randolph B. Marcy, faced with crossing the Pecos country later in 1849 en route from Santa Fe, New Mexico, to Fort Smith, Arkansas, by way of El Paso, noted that "as several parties had reached El Paso from Texas, I was satisfied I could go through."[5]

In his 1849-1850 survey of the general route of the Emigrant Road, U.S. Army topographical engineer N. H. Michler, Jr., found the hundreds of miles from Fort Washita to present Big Spring "almost a perfect level, well watered the greater portion, and well timbered. . . . A more advantageous country for roads of any kind cannot be found."[6] Brad C. Fowler, a member of the Rhine wagon-train party of 1853, concurred, calling it "one of the best natural roads in the world."[7]

Beyond Big Spring, however, the arid wilderness of the Pecos loomed formidable. "The sand hills, and the scarcity of wood and water, from the 'Big springs' to the Pecos, form the only objection . . . ," Michler wrote. "The grass was indifferent, and the soil poor and unproductive." He found the Pecos at Emigrant Crossing so barren that only a "line of high reeds" marked its banks. Adjacent to it, meanwhile, lay "numerous lakes" with water even more repulsive than that of the Pecos.[8]

Although Michler and his command camped at Emigrant on December 30, 1849, they chose not to cross, intimidated by the deep, forty-foot-wide "rolling mass of red mud."[9] A few early cartographers drew upon such descriptions in designating the ford "Red River Crossing"[10]—a term that, like the reported alternate name of "Outlaw Crossing,"[11] foreshadowed the bloodshed to follow.

Whatever its name, the crossing and its approaching road remained demanding for succeeding westbound travelers. In travers-ing the "great Sandy Desert" between Big Spring and the Pecos in the summer of 1853, Fowler of the Rhine party was stunned by the abundance of wagon irons and horse and cattle skeletons marking the dunes. "We are struck with pain and sorrow at the destructive sight . . . ," he wrote, "to which number we added our skeletons of animals by hundreds."

By comparison, even sinister Emigrant Crossing was a wel-come sight to Fowler, who dubbed the Pecos "the most handsome lit-tle stream I ever saw."[12]

U. S. Army Brevet Captain John Pope, however, did noth-ing but curse the ford upon reaching it March 24, 1854, during his survey of a proposed transcontinental railroad route. "Emigrant Crossing . . . ," he wrote, " is an extremely bad crossing; our oxen swam for upwards of thirty feet to the opposite bank." He stressed that it would be "utterly impossible" for wagons to cross without fer-rying, as the ford presented "many difficulties—soft bottom, deep stream, and on the east side miry banks."[13]

Conditions at Emigrant Crossing, however, may have varied seasonally, dictated by floods. Barney Hubbs, at the site half a century later, remembered it as a "good crossing" where a draw, intersecting from the southwest, deposited sand and gravel to form a "hard crust in the bed of the river."[14] Regardless, from the mid-1800s on, stalwart pioneers headed west to face the challenge not only of the river but also of the sun-scorched land through which it snaked.

The McCulloch party of 1858 endured an ordeal that rivaled even that of the Strentzel group. Leaving Dallas on April 12 with eleven wagons, forty-seven yoke of oxen, and 1600 head of cattle, the emigrants—upon reaching old Camp Johnston near present-day Carlsbad, Texas—turned upstream along the little-traveled North Concho River instead of continuing southward to the better-known Middle Concho. It almost cost them their lives. From the North Concho's headwater springs, eleven miles northwest of present-day Sterling City, they struck out across a dry, unknown country in the hope of hitting the Pecos at Horsehead Crossing. Soon realizing they had missed the road that stretched west from the Middle Concho to Horsehead, they nevertheless forged on, guided only by a compass.

On the third morning of travel across the waterless stretch, the famishing cattle smelled water and increased their gait. Pushing on in advance of the wagons, the drovers pressed the herd throughout the day and all that night, and at daybreak they struck the Emigrant Road fifteen miles east of the sandhills. The herd immediately stampeded, running eight miles along the road before turning north into deep sand drifts. For four hours the drovers fought desperately to turn the beeves back onto the road before succeeding, only to leave 550 head dead or dying of thirst.

By now, the herd had gone almost seventy-six hours without water and had traveled nearly 130 miles. The drovers, meanwhile, had been in the saddle almost thirty straight hours, during which time not a drop of water had crossed their lips. Near death, they had no choice but to do the ordinarily unthinkable.

"Many shot down the famishing bullocks on the road, stuck them, pulled off their shoes or boots, caught the thick hot blood and drank it freely, and by so doing saved their lives," party member William Curless wrote on July 3.

Finally, at 4:00 p.m. on the fourth day without water, they stumbled across "weak alkali" pools in the sandhills. Still, five lagging drovers would have died had not others ridden ahead and returned with full canteens.

Meanwhile, the trailing wagoners faced their own ordeal; water was rationed to a pint per person per day. Further peril came as the wagons approached within thirty miles of the sandhills—the work oxen smelled water and went mad with thirst, forcing the wagoners to unyoke the animals and start them along the herd trail. Their drovers, subjected to intense thirst and fatigue, soon feared for their own lives and returned to the stranded wagons, leaving the oxen to push on alone. Only twelve head ever made it to the pools and cattle herd; the other eighty died or strayed in the sands.

When communication finally opened between the herd camp and the wagon train, the dehydrated women and children were carried to the alkali pools, where awaited only six yoke of exhausted oxen to outfit eleven wagons. Desperation forced the emigrants to rig new teams by yoking wild steers.

Thirty-two miles later, the party reached Emigrant Crossing on the Pecos, a "narrow, deep, winding ditch of a stream," wrote Curless. Struggling on to El Paso, Curless (in his July 3, 1858, letter to the *Dallas Herald*) issued a dire warning against challenging the North Concho-to-Emigrant Crossing route. "Only one train in a hundred can make the trip," he said.[15]

Seventy-five days afterward, the first Butterfield Overland Mail stage rumbled past Emigrant Crossing and on up the east side of the Pecos en route from Tipton, Missouri, to San Francisco. About 10:00 p.m. on September 26, driver Henry Skillman halted the stage for the night at a station consisting of an adobe corral and an adobe house still under construction.[16] Although designated "Emigrant Crossing Station," the station actually lay at a point known as the "Narrows," thirteen miles upstream of the ford.[17]

The threat of Indian attack was an ever-present scythe hanging over the station.

"The three Americans in charge of the station had . . . calculated that they could defend the stock against a whole tribe of Indians," wrote Waterman Ormsby, the only through passenger on the first westbound stage. "This seemed to be the only fear at any of these stations—that the Indians would steal the stock. . . . Several had been seen in the vicinity."[18]

The crossing likewise came under the threat of Indians—Comanches through the early 1870s, Apaches until 1881. With

*Jeff Glass. (Sparkman Collection,
in possession of author)*

Indians stealing cattle from nearby ranches in the spring of 1879, Colonel George A. Armes embarked April 7 on a long scout from Fort Stockton, thirty-five miles south-southeast of Emigrant Crossing. May 6 found Armes and his command at the ford, where they rested two hours before resuming their thirty-two-mile march of that day. Armes did not report Indian signs at Emigrant, but he considered the threat of attack in the immediate area so great that, at camp on the Pecos that night, he refused to permit a campfire.[19]

Hostiles no longer threatened by 1885 when twenty-four-year-old Jeff Glass drove a herd of longhorns for James B. Hiler from the North Concho River southwestward to Presidio County. Nevertheless, Glass learned firsthand why the Pecos was hated and feared. Denied by Texas & Pacific Railroad officials the opportunity to water the herd at the fledgling settlement of Odessa, Glass and trail boss Ryfe Ridley could only push the beeves on toward the Pecos. Crazed by thirst, many of the animals scattered and dropped out of the herd, forcing the cowboys to leave them behind in order to save the balance. Upon finally nearing the Pecos—likely at Emigrant Crossing—the drovers held the herd well away from the river and took only small bunches at a time down to water.

Sent back to pick up the strays, Glass drove the weakened animals on to the river, where he swam the herd across in a desperate, frenzied push. In his journal, only eight days before, he had noted, "A lonesome time on the plains twenty miles west of Midland on herd." But now, even the bleak, melancholy prairie seemed a paradise. "Yes, indeed, you may call the plains lonesome," he wrote from the banks of the river on July 24, 1885, "but this ___damned Pecos River is a SB of a place."[20]

*Barney Hubbs. (courtesy, West of
the Pecos Museum, Pecos, Texas)*

In 1908, eleven-year-old Barney Hubbs and his parents, forced from their North Concho River ranch in a sheepman-cowman dispute, drove their six hundred head of cattle west to Emigrant Crossing and a homestead upstream.

"I drove the chuckwagon," recalled Hubbs more than eight decades later. "We were sixteen days on the road driving cattle across. . . . You can't drive cattle but eight or ten miles a day because they've got to eat as they go along. . . . There was one barbed wire fence between the Pecos River and San Angelo at that time. We followed no road or anything; we'd just head for the Pecos River and Emigrant Crossing. That was the crossing that we had been directed to hit."

In late January or early February, Hubbs pulled the chuckwagon to a halt where the crossing's bare banks suddenly fell away without warning.

"Regular flow at that time was around three or four feet deep at Emigrant Crossing, which was a little bit high for our wagon," said Hubbs, who remembered swimming the cattle to the west bank. "They had logs, cottonwood logs there . . . on both sides of the river, that you'd tie on to the wheels of the wagon and float the wagon across. The emigrants did that [left the logs], back yonder."[21]

Fences and bridges had ended Emigrant Crossing's history as a public ford by the 1920s, but cowboys such as Jim Witt still splashed across it regularly on horseback or by wagon. Born in 1914, Witt grew up on the Cross C Ranch, which encompassed the crossing and seventeen miles of east river front below the present U.S. Highway 80 bridge. He forded Emigrant for the first time in the summer of 1926 or 1927 in order to camp and break horses at the nearby Bateman Ranch, then under lease to the Cross C.

"It was shallow, less than knee-deep to a horse," he recalled in 1993. "It was a little bit gravelly; it wasn't boggy. You could still see those old wagon tracks, pretty deep, washed out. Those banks were pretty straight up and down on both sides [upstream and down-stream] of it, and there was salt cedars and some pretty good-sized mesquite bushes."

Witt and other Cross C cowboys frequently used Emigrant to push stray cattle back to the river's east side.

"Cattle would walk across there and go to the Bateman well half a mile to get a drink of water, because it was real good water," he remembered. "They wouldn't drink that ol' river water when they knew that Bateman well water was over there. So we crossed there all the time. See, we had to swim the horse if we wanted to cross the river anywhere on that ranch except Emigrant Crossing and Rocky Crossing [upstream near the U.S. 80 bridge]."[22]

No one knows how many pioneers faced the miry east bank[23] at Emigrant; its registry consisted of only wagon ruts and horse paths. But its shores are haunted by the memory of one party whose story, long forgotten, resurfaced decades later with the discovery of post-mortem evidence. Yet, as astounding as the find was, the full story of these foredoomed travelers remains frustratingly mired in conjecture and a secondhand account.

Barney Hubbs, Earl Ligon, and Louis Roberson at Emigrant Crossing. (courtesy, Clayton Wheat Williams Collection, N. S. Haley Memorial Library, Midland, Texas)

By the term of Reeves County Sheriff E. B. Kiser (who served from 1918 to 1930),[24] the southwest bank of Emigrant Crossing had been swallowed up by the ranch of Earl Ligon. In about 1924, on a lonely, thirty-five-foot bluff sentineling the Pecos three-quarters of a mile downstream of the ford,[25] Ligon stumbled upon a human skull and took it to the sheriff's office. Suspecting foul play, Sheriff Kiser and Deputy Louis Roberson undertook an investigation and permitted a man named Hill and Barney Hubbs to participate; Hubbs, by that time, was a newspaper man in the town of Pecos, eighteen miles west of Emigrant Crossing.[26]

"We got a party up, some Mexicans to do the digging, and we went down there," recalled Hubbs in 1992. "And these Mexicans dug up eighteen skeletons, just a mass burial there. . . . They had been just stuffed in there, you know, no protection on the bodies. . . . The coyotes had dug up their skeletons. . . . I don't think there was any children in the bunch; we dug them up some, but there was no children in the bunch that we could find."[27]

Realizing the skeletons did not represent a recent mass murder, Sheriff Kiser instructed that the remains be reburied. Still, the investigators were faced with a great mystery. What had happened here to claim the lives of so many individuals, all of whom had been laid to rest in a common grave?

Nearby, Hubbs and the lawmen found important clues which suggested that a wagon train had burned at the site. Said Hubbs, "The iron work off the wagons was still there . . . the wagon rims."[28]

Too, the men considered the proximity of Emigrant Crossing—only 1,300 or so yards away—and the fact that Indian depredations had been common in the region through the 1870s. And suddenly the discovery took on considerable significance: it suggested one of the largest massacres by Indians in Texas history,[29] larger than the infamous massacre of seven men with the Warren wagon train in Young County in 1871, larger even than the loss of sixteen persons to Comanches and Kiowas at Howard's Well in the lower Pecos country in 1872.[30]

Noted Hubbs: "The supposition is—and most of it *is* supposition—that . . . they were emigrants, and they were crossing the river at Emigrant Crossing, and the Indians attacked them and killed [them] all. . . . They took everything they wanted in the way of bedding and blankets and so forth, then just burned the rest . . . and left the bodies out on the ground."[31]

Firm documentation of what really happened to those eighteen persons eluded Hubbs and investigating officers, but oral statements, recorded decades later, at least gave clues, albeit shaky. Petroleum engineer A. B. Kelley reported to historian Clayton Williams that W. H. Abrams, of the Land Department of Texas & Pacific Railway, had told him the following:

In the 1870s, Murray Harris and his T&P Railway Company survey crew, accompanied by army troops, met a party of westbound emigrants a day's ride east of the Pecos and warned them of hostile Indians in the area. Unwilling to delay their journey until the troops could furnish escort, the emigrants continued on. The next day, the troops and surveyors forded Emigrant Crossing to find, and bury, their scalped and mutilated bodies.[32]

Indeed, army records verify that such surveys did take place under military guard. In the summer of 1872, Captain Edward M. Heyl and companies from the Eleventh Infantry and Fourth Cavalry accompanied a T&P survey crew pushing west for the Pecos.[33] The following spring, L. E. Edwards and J. A. McMillan dispatched a letter to the commander at Fort Stockton:

"Having to make a survey of the Pecos River from the Melville Station [Camp Melvin] on Fickland Crossing [Pontoon

The mass grave near Emigrant Crossing. (author)

Crossing] to when said river reaches the southern line of New Mexico . . . in locating lands for the Texas and Central Railroad, I hereby make application for an escort of at least six infantry troops with transportation for fifty days."[34]

On April 2, 1873, the Eleventh Infantry and Company K, Fourth Cavalry, marched out of Fort Stockton en route to the Pecos to escort the surveyors,[35] identified in post returns for March and April as associated with the "Texas and Pacific Railroad."[36] By July 6, the surveyors had worked their way upstream to a point above Horsehead Crossing, where Captain Charles A. Wikoff and his company joined the party.

"I reached Horsehead Crossing . . . and found the ford impassable for loaded wagons in consequence of the swollen condition of the river, and [learned] that the surveying party were in camp seven miles above on the opposite side," Wikoff reported. "Mr. Muscriss [or Muscriff], the engineer in charge, rode down to my camp in the evening and informed me that . . . our route will be from Horsehead Crossing up the Pecos River about one hundred miles to the mouth of Delaware Creek."

From that point, Wikoff noted, the surveyors intended to veer west for the Guadalupe Mountains and establish camp within forty miles of Fort Bliss (at present El Paso) "about the end of August."[37]

The surveyors kept close to schedule and passed Emigrant Crossing in July, for on July 28 a Major Hurd of the party—evidently reaching the departure point on the Pecos—requested one sergeant and ten cavalry troopers for the trek to the Guadalupes. [38] Nevertheless, in the modern historian's search for proof of a massacre at Emigrant Crossing during that month or any other, extant Fort Stockton records are as silent as the skulls themselves.

Another version of the legend, meanwhile—based on the reported testimony of a former Fort Davis buffalo soldier known as "Old Nigger George"—implies that the skeletons were of an Indian war party. Destroying a wagon train in the sandhills near present Monahans, the Indians supposedly fled a pursuing Fort Stockton army patrol only to be overtaken at the crossing and killed.[39] The account suggests a tie-in with the Willow Springs Massacre, a legend charging that Indians slaughtered an emigrant party and burned its wagons in free-drifting dunes near later Old Flag Mill, eleven miles northeast of Monahans.[40]

The Emigrant Crossing victims, whether Indian or pioneer, were destined to fade unnamed into history, and only jumbled rocks atop that forlorn bluff memorialize their passing.[41] Similarly, Emigrant Crossing has been all but forgotten, lying peacefully secluded today in the H&GN Survey of Reeves County, Block 7, B. Calahan Section 1. Salt cedars now choke its once-barren banks, and dams upstream at Red Bluff Lake and in New Mexico have reduced its "rolling mass of red mud" to a polluted creep.

Decades after he had crossed Emigrant as an eleven-year-old, Barney Hubbs returned to look for signs of a bygone era.

"The Pecos got very low, water-wise, and the bed of the river became visible, and three or four of us went down there to Emigrant Crossing and took pictures . . .," he recalled. "The wagon tracks were still visible in the bed of the river. . . . Of course, down through the years, the salt cedar trees and everything [had] . . . just about covered the river up, but the crossing was still visible across the river if you looked at it close enough."[43]

In 1993, Hubbs died—one last link to the history of emigrant passage at the ford, while time and nature still continue steadfast in slowly erasing this landmark from the face of the West. ★

Emigrant Crossing as seen today from downstream. (author)

Cattlemen called the Pecos a graveyard.[1] Buffalo hunters likened the river to hell.[2] And in all its nine hundred miles, westering pioneers feared most a yards-wide span that early traveler Stephen Powers judged "the very abode and throne of death."[3]

Grotesque with skulls—horse, steer, even human— Horsehead Crossing was the Old West's most-dreaded ford, the place of judgment for men and animals already lured seventy-five miles west through a waterless hell that history would know as a stretch of the Comanche war trail, Upper Road, Butterfield stage line, or Goodnight-Loving Trail.

"I hope that I may never experience the want of water again, or witness the like suffering that our men and Horses endured," mourned wagoner C. C. Cox upon reaching Horsehead in 1849.[4]

"Thousands upon thousands of cattle lay dead about the Pecos, while all the road was white with fleshless bones," found Powers in 1868.[5]

"We can see the dead cattle floating down while we are dipping up the water and see them lying on the banks all over," lamented emigrant Ruth Shackleford the same year. "This is all we will have to drink for 87 miles."[6]

Lying twelve miles west-southwest of the gateway pass of Castle Gap[7] and thirteen miles southwest of modern Crane, Horsehead nurtured death and violence as early as the 1700s, when Comanches from the headwaters of the Arkansas and Red rivers first splashed across on horseback en route to Mexico and haciendas ripe for plunder.[8] In 1859, as passenger Albert D. Richardson's westbound Butterfield Overland Mail stage rumbled away from the ford, he committed to memory the "eight beaten paths side by side [which] indicated the frequency of their bloody raids into northern Mexico, for cattle, horses, and children."[9] Pushing the stolen horses hard back across a final sixty miles of desert, Comanches or Kiowas regained Horsehead only to see the thirst-crazed animals sometimes plunge into the water and drink until they died.[10] The hideous skulls marked the crossing for years, giving birth to a name synonymous with the history and legends of the West.

"Back in the [eighteen] eighties . . . an old Mexican . . . named Elezaro Mendillas . . . told me that when he was a boy he was there and they still had horse heads sticking up in the . . . [scrub brush] on both sides of the river," related James W. Mullens in 1927. "He said that they kept the practice up. When one fell down someone else would come along and put it up."[11]

In 1849, the skulls greeted gold-hungry argonauts as they forged west on the Upper Road in their stampede for California. [12] Among the wagoners were Cox and Lewis B. Harris, who set out "for the New El Dorado" from a town near Houston on April 14. Taking up with a wagon train in Fredericksburg,[13] they pressed on into a wilderness that, from the headwaters of the Middle Concho River

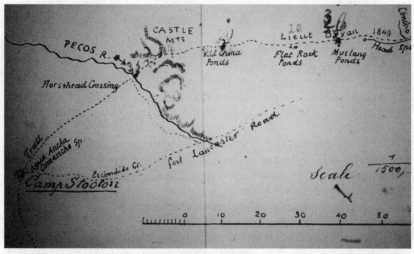

First Lieutenant Fred W. Smith's October 1867 field map showing the route (marked "Lieut. Bryan 1849") from the Middle Concho to Castle Gap and Horsehead Crossing. (National Archives)

west, degenerated into "a perfect waste. . . ," Cox wrote in his diary June 3. "I never saw the earth so dry as it is in this district, vegetation is completely burned up, and every water hole is dry as a `bone yard.' . . . The weather has been oppressive, and the dust upon the road almost suffocating."[14]

Forced to travel the desert day and night to survive, the wagoners navigated Castle Gap's mile-long pass by dark. Wrote Harris: "It was a most magnificent sight to see the long train of wagons and pack mules, winding their way through the pass by moonlight, the rocks almost overhanging them on either side, and towering up, hundreds of feet into the sky, every object almost appearing ready to transform itself into an indignant Comanche or Apache, ready to roll the rocks upon our heads for changing their long used war trail into a smooth wagon road."[15]

Upon crossing the Pecos at Horsehead on June 3 and heading upstream, the emigrants tarried only long enough to curse the river and its environs.

"It is certainly a lonesome looking place," observed Cox, "a vast plain with nothing to relieve the view but the distant dismal mountains to the east and south which rise like bulwarks upon the sea. . . . The bones of many a noble horse lay whitening upon the earth . . . . There is not a breath of wind, and the sun, always powerful, is rendered doubly intense by the reflection from the sand."[16]

Harris was even more damning: "[I] would not pay taxes on a league of it, if the government would donate the balance of it to me. We have had nothing but one steady stream of dust and sand since we struck it, and the sand now covers my ink as I write."[17]

With Horsehead so unpredictable that the depth of its rushing waters would "change every hour," according to George Owens, who crossed with the Twenty-Fourth U.S. Infantry in 1873,[18] wagoners faced potential disaster every time they urged their teams into the currents. Fording proved a test not only of mettle but also of inventiveness. When fifty men and twenty families reached Horsehead with thirty wagons in 1857, they formed a crude ferry by lashing empty water barrels to the bed of a wagon hitched with four yoke of oxen.

"With two men on either side of the oxen and one on either side of the wagon to keep it from upsetting, they swam back and forth until they had crossed all the women and children and men that could not swim, and all supplies," emigrant Rachel Eads related fifty-six years later. "My sister and myself were brave enough to cross on the first load, and as we found nothing for fuel but small sage roots, we set to digging roots and making coffee for the poor chilled men when they came over."[19]

No point along the Pecos was more infamous for Indian attack than Horsehead, where the mere threat of hostilities moved travelers to extraordinary acts. On July 25, 1858, the westbound Oscar Call party, upon traversing the last few miles of hot sand and watching the thirsty horses dive off the steep banks, grew concerned about Indian signs.

"We found at the crossing where the Indians had killed five or six horses for food," wrote Call in his diary. "Heaps of bones lay around the old camp fires as though they were used for fuel."

Forced to camp at the ford to rest their horses, the men kept a sharp lookout, because, said Call, "the moon is nearly full and a marauding party will probably pass in a day or two on their way to or from Mexico."

About midnight, sudden uneasiness in their horses alarmed the men. "Our horses . . . kept looking in the direction of the other side of the river," wrote Call. "I presently saw several [strange] horses come down the bank to the river, and immediately after, two more came charging down the river bank. . . . One of their tails was trimmed Indian fashion. . . . Doc thought that he saw some one driving them."

Though the Indian horses disappeared without incident, it was a portent of things to come. Sleeping but little, the men pushed upstream the next day and camped again on the river bank. Building a fire at dusk "in a hole where it could not be seen thirty steps," they cooked and ate supper in silence. As they went to secure their horses, the dark across the river suddenly burst into flames.

"The Indians had fired the grass . . . and it was burning rapidly . . . ," detailed Call. "We hastily tied our horses and, taking our rifles, sat down by a cluster of mesquite bushes, expecting an attack."

They kept up the vigil on into midnight, when they heard the sudden neighing of horses upstream. Concluding that it was a war party waiting to attack at daybreak, the desperate men huddled in a quiet "council of war," related Call, "and agreed to fall back to the [Castle] mountains before daylight where we could fight them on our own terms."

Quietly saddling their mounts, they struck out through the

dark for Castle Gap and the safety of settlements far to the east.[20]

Although the Pecos was without a significant military deterrent during much of the Civil War and for two years afterward, by 1865 Texas cowmen looked to the Indian-plagued river for passage to New Mexico markets. In October of that year, trail boss Bob Wylie and twenty-four drovers headed out for the Pecos from Palo Pinto County and the Brazos River with two herds that included 3,200 steers contracted to the government at Fort Sumner, New Mexico.

"The herd was made up by many men putting in cattle—I. W. Cox and Bob Wylie were two of these. . . ," recalled drover Irbin H. Bell in 1927. "We went a little south of west and struck the [Middle] Concho River. We came up the Concho and crossed the plains to the Horsehead. . . . We came through Castle Gap on the way to Horsehead Crossing, having a ninety-mile dry drive. We lost no cattle, but drove pretty near all the time on that stretch. . . . Just before we got through the gap, the cattle smelled the water from the river and we had to hold them back—there were alkali pools to guard against."

With Horsehead attained without mishap, five or so drovers set off back toward the Brazos while the remainder threw the herds together and proceeded up the Pecos to Fort Sumner. Said Bell:

"We saw no sign of a wagon or anything up the Pecos. . . . There were lots of buffalo in sight to the east, watering at the river. There were some west of the Pecos, but they did not stay on that side much. We stayed on the east side all the way up. . . . [We] were gone about four months, getting back in February."[22]

The success of Wylie and other trail bosses in driving herds from the Brazos country to Horsehead and up to Fort Sumner cleared the way for Oliver Loving to make his own plans known by letter May 22, 1866: "I have about one thousand cattle under herd and expect to start to the mountains between the first and fifth of next month."[23] By summer's end, Loving and his partner, Charles Goodnight, not only had pushed a herd over the same general trail, but also had brought it such recognition that historians would label it the Goodnight-Loving Trail.

More often than not during late 1866 and 1867, blood spilled by Indian attack marked the course, especially at Horsehead Crossing. Less than a month after the U.S. Army reoccupied Fort Stockton thirty-four miles southwest on July 7, 1867,[24] post commander Edward Hatch noted in a dispatch the importance of guarding Horsehead when cattle "intended for government use in New Mexico" approached.

"During the last year," he wrote, "I am informed that every drove of cattle intended for the posts of New Mexico were captured when passing this place [Horsehead]. . . . The last drove would have undoubtedly been captured if it were not for the timely discovery of the Indian trail and rapid marching of Captain [George H.] Gamble."[25]

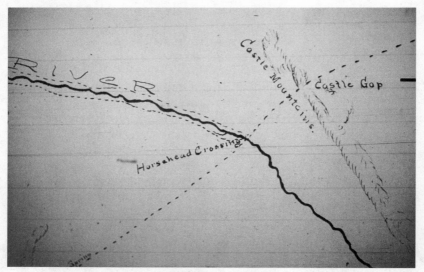

Captain George Gamble's field map of his September-October 1867 scout to Horsehead Crossing. (National Archives)

In fact, Gamble, returning to report that "the Pecos River appears to be the range of all the Indians in this part of the country," recommended Horsehead Crossing for "a post to protect the New Mexico road"[26]—a suggestion the army did not heed.

Likewise, First Lieutenant Fred W. Smith's October 22, 1867, recommendation that the army span the crossing with a bridge went ignored. Seeking timber on the Concho River for building purposes at Fort Stockton, Smith learned firsthand that Horsehead loomed as a major obstacle to wagons bearing lumber.

"The road crosses a very bad point on the Pecos—Horsehead Crossing—[with] . . . sudden rising . . . [and] almost irresistible current, when so risen . . . ," he reported. "I found the river very high, my wagon remaining fast for nearly half an hour in the water, thereby spoiling nearly half of my rations, all of my sugar, salt, pepper, and obliging me to put my new men on half rations during the march and to allow them to expend their ammunition in killing game."[27]

Meanwhile, emigrants faced the threat not only of the river, but also of hostiles. "The old Butterfield Overland stage route [is] now much used by emigrants," noted outgoing correspondence from Fort Stockton headquarters on August 31. "The road to Fort Sumner and New Mexico up the Pecos . . . looks to this post for its protection at its most dangerous point, Horse Head Crossing."[28]

Despite the perils, one wagon train after another rolled west in June 1868 over the Butterfield branch that ran from Horsehead to Forts Davis and Stockton and points beyond. In one week of travel in the Trans-Pecos late that month, Ruth Shackleford and her party—returning disillusioned from California—met five wagon trains headed for what she sarcastically termed "the land of gold, they think."[29]

One of the caravans may have included Stephen Powers, whose remarkable 3,556-mile journey by foot from Raleigh, North Carolina, to San Francisco in 1868 found him laboring that very month through Castle Gap—a "pass of peril, of awful and sublime grandeur," he called it. With thirst raging and the Pecos still hours away, he emerged from the gap after nightfall on the third sleepless night and somehow pushed ahead of the wagons. In the sandy flat stretching twelve miles to the Pecos, he overtook the drags of the advance cattle herd and struggled alongside, making but a step at a time, just as they did.

"The weaker ones, maddened by thirst, with eyes sunken and fiercely glaring, were . . . reeling along in the moonlight," he wrote. "One of them made a desperate lunge at me, and I avoided it barely in time to see him plunge headlong, and bury his head deep in the sand."

Weak from exhaustion and sleep deprivation, Powers, too, finally succumbed. "I struggled desperately . . . ," he wrote, "but it was of no use, and finally I lay sprawled upon the sand, helpless as any capsized turtle. A crazy steer made a pass at me, but stumbled and missed, and we lay there side by side."

Picked up by a passing wagoner, Powers finally gained Horsehead during the night to watch the driver unyoke the famished oxen. "As each poor fellow was released," Powers related, "we could see him wobble away in the dim moonlight, and see his tail whisk at the moon as he went over the bank with a stupendous souse.

"Then every man made a run for the Pecos, and the amount of water which we drank was astonishing. Though it was thick with red clay, we all agreed that it was the sweetest we ever drank."

Despite its life-giving waters, Horsehead by daylight proved "appalling in its ghastliness," said Powers. "Many great droves had arrived before us . . . . Some of the frenzied animals had rushed head-long into the glittering pools of alkali, and quaffed the crystal death, falling where they stood. The Pecos has absolutely no valley and no trees, but wriggles right through the midst of the plain, which is hideous with bleaching skeletons. . . . It swept down in its swift and swirling flood, innumerable cattle and horses, which had struggled so bravely and so uncomplainingly only to perish at the last."

Resting at the river several days—during which Powers retraced by foot the stretch he had traveled by wagon—the emi-grants grimly counted their cattle losses: "Of those magnificent herds which swept out so lordly upon the Staked Plain, with their long and swinging stride," reported Powers, "twelve hundred head lay dead along the Pecos, or fed their festering flesh to its waves."[30]

On June 26 at Fort Stockton, the eastbound Shackleford wagon train split, with several wagoners choosing the Lower Road—which crossed the Pecos near old Fort Lancaster—rather than facing the wasteland between Horsehead and the Middle Concho. Despite the waiting desert, Ruth Shackleford, her husband, Frank, and four-teen other men and their families pushed on and made camp June 28 on the west bank of Horsehead, which she described in her diary as "nasty, dirty, muddy, ugly. . . . Everything within two or three miles around is burned up with alkali and the dead cattle lay thick on the banks of the river. . . . They have to take the horses two miles from camp to get grass."[31] Fortunately for the Shackleford party—and for drovers who rested two thousand cattle on the east bank[32]—a Fort Stockton picket had deterred Indian attack since setting up stakes at the crossing in April or earlier.[33]

Nevertheless, the Pecos bred other unpleasantries that the army could do nothing about. "The mosquitos lost no time last night in keeping me company," Ruth wrote on June 29. "The boys around camp had to sit up all night with blankets wrapped over their heads and keep smoking to keep them from eating their eyes out. The guards had to smoke their pipes and even then were almost eaten up by them. The horses are covered with knots where they have been bitten."

With daybreak came other discomfort. Wrote Ruth, "I have to cook all day in the hot sun. . . . There is not the least bit of shade to put our horses under. The little children are crying because the sun burns them and they can't get out of it."

Meanwhile, the men crossed each wagon by swimming the river and pulling the vehicle across by rope tied to the tongue. They relied on a raft improvised from water barrels for cargo transport until the infantrymen supplied a skiff, which later served to ferry the women and children across.

Pressing on to the east the next day for Castle Gap—where, they had been told, three thousand cattle carcasses lay rotting—the emigrants found death sentineling them all the way. Wrote Ruth:

"We came fifteen miles through a doleful looking country with alkali dust three or four inches deep. Every now and then we would pass a pile of dead cattle seven or eight in a pile . . . . We came through the long dreaded canyon [Castle Gap] but did not have half as much use for our camphor as we expected to. There were about three hundred dead cattle from the river up."[34]

On the afternoon of July 1, the Shackleford party met a west-bound cattle herd[35]—possibly that of William Hinton Posey, who drove to California over the Butterfield route that year. Reaching Horsehead Crossing and resting his herd, Posey penned a quick letter to his wife on July 4: "I am on the Pecos. We have had a terrible time. We crossed the Plains without finding any water, a distance of eighty-five miles. Some few of our stock starved."[36]

Brothers D. H. and J. W. Snyder, punching a mixed herd up the Goodnight-Loving Trail in 1869, negotiated the dry stretch in seventy hours by driving day and night, a method employed by nearly all discerning trail bosses. At the normal pace of a drive, the waterless ordeal between the Middle Concho and Pecos would have required five to seven days—a death sentence to even the strongest steer, an animal accustomed to watering daily.

"In crossing the dry stretch . . . ," detailed D. N. Arnett, who took a herd up the Pecos to New Mexico and across to California the same year, "we watered our cattle out on the Concho in the afternoon about 2:00 p.m. It was the next day, and the next, before getting to water [at Horsehead]. We would drive at night until the cattle wanted to lie down. They would rest awhile and then get up and go to milling around, and we would start with them again."[38]

Even if drovers successfully navigated the desert, they still faced disaster at Horsehead's sheer banks.

"The country through the Castle Gap canyon was sort of damp and seepy, and the cattle gave us trouble getting through," recalled Arnett in 1926. "But soon after getting out, the cattle smelled the water on the Pecos and went into it like turtles off a log."[39]

Often, drovers could do nothing but ride on and leave scores of beeves and horses to die in the quicksands below the river's sudden walls. On at least one occasion, however, the tendency of thirsty animals to plunge off the banks had humorous consequences.

"I helped take a herd to the Pecos in 1869 . . . ," related C. J. White in 1928. "There were 4,500 head in it . . . from Coryell County. When the cattle got to where they could smell the river after the long dry drive, they made a rush for it. The little Mexican mules that were hitched to the chuckwagon made a run too, and they went off over the bank at a run. There was a man in the *cuña*, the cowhide swung under the wagon for carrying wood. He was there asleep, and they ran off and went in with him. He floated out and he came up downstream a ways, as mad as could be."[40]

In the fall of 1869, seventeen-year-old W. C. Cochran and ten other drovers, driving 1,500 cattle to Horsehead and up the Pecos to Colorado, found day-old Indian signs in Castle Gap but eluded attack.[41] Irbin H. Bell and Frank Cowden were not as fortunate in August of 1870 when they headed out for Fort Sumner with approximately 1,500 beeves. On the plain east of Castle Gap, they came upon burned wagons and the remnant of a herd stampeded by Indians. Undaunted, Bell and Cowden forged on to Horsehead and pointed the herd upstream, where they soon struck up an acquaintance with Ed Walker, who bossed a second northbound drove. Twelve miles above the crossing, the men bedded their herds about three hundred yards apart and positioned their remudas in between.

"After midnight, a big black cloud came up and it looked like it was going to rain," recalled Bell in 1927. "The Indians came in and stampeded our cattle. The horses and cattle could smell the Indians and were ready to stampede anyway. The horses began to snort and rear when they smelled them, and both herds scattered then. The Indians picked up a hundred head of our cattle and we had barely enough horses to get along with."

Picking up the Indians' trail, Bell and five other men pursued the Indians toward rugged hills north of Castle Gap. "We went about eight or ten miles through some very rough country," related Bell. "When I told the boys that we had come far enough, that we would run into the Indians in the canyons and they would kill us all, we went back to the herd and drove on to Fort Sumner."[42]

That same month, emigrant Maria Shrode and her party fortunately avoided hostiles in gaining Horsehead and turning upstream, but the "bones of dead cattle strewed round in every direction" in Castle Gap testified to the perils of the Pecos desert.[43]

A. D. Cantrell learned of the dangers intimately when he helped drive a herd to Horsehead and upstream to Fort Sumner about 1871. "Seemed like death stalked right along with us . . . ," he recalled decades later. "Two boys with a herd just ahead of us got to quarreling, drew their guns and zip, zip, first one and then the other fell. We buried them . . . on the plains just this side of Castle Mountain. Then we went on our way . . . and we found a man who had been killed by the Comanches. . . . We buried the fellow, and in a little while we caught up with a Negro . . . [who] had been with the dead man when the redskins got him, but had outridden them."

Driving up the Pecos, Cantrell and the drovers not only encountered Indians and lost all their horses—which they fortunately recovered—but also came close to losing the entire cattle herd to stampede. Said Cantrell: "It was pouring rain, dark as pitch and cold as the north pole. . . . Off they ran, with us in front of them for eight miles, when they finally slowed down to a trot. We began shooting off our guns and soon had them quieted down. . . . When daylight came . . . we set out to find the wanderers and came upon them in a lake about ten miles away, near an [abandoned] Indian camp."[44]

Twenty-year-old Columbus Fleming Barton avoided Indian confrontation in Texas during his 1872 drive from San Saba County to Horsehead and north to Pueblo, Colorado, but disaster struck about fifty miles from Fort Sumner. "The Indians stole our horses," he related in 1941. "We drove the cattle two hundred fifty miles afoot. I wore my boots out, cut the tops off, and wrapped around the soles. Had to stand guard at night among the rattlesnakes afoot."[45]

G. W. Roberson, taking a herd to Tucson, Arizona, by way of Horsehead Crossing in 1873, met with adversity long before gaining the Pecos. Readying the cattle for the long push west from the Middle Concho, Roberson and his fellow drovers came under Indian attack about sundown. "They began shooting at us and chased off about thirty-five head of our horses, which left us almost afoot," he recalled in 1926. "We gave them a running fight of about four miles, but it had been a hard day around the herd and our horses were played out, so they ran off and left us. We killed one Indian that we knew of, and captured four head of their horses with saddles on.

"The Indians used both pistols and bows and arrows in the fight. There were about twelve or fifteen in our outfit, and quite a lot of our boys had to walk and drive. The raid left us with less than one horse apiece and we had just about enough to keep the herd thrown together and pointed."[46]

Such depredations against cattle droves prompted Captain F. S. Dodge of Fort Stockton, on May 13, 1873, to declare the country unsafe "from Johnson's Station, twenty-five miles west of Fort Concho, to Seven Rivers in New Mexico." Although conceding that "perhaps this cavalry here [at Fort Stockton] cannot be better employed than in this duty [of escorting herds]," he noted that "if the same number of herds are driven over the road this season that have passed in previous years, it would take half a regiment to furnish the required [cavalry] details."[47]

In August 1874, with Comanches and Kiowas riding the war trail one last time before Colonel Ranald Mackenzie destroyed their rancherias and crushed their spirit in the Texas Panhandle, Second Lieutenant Thomas Davenport of Fort Stockton successfully escorted a drove up the Pecos. Presumably, Davenport and his eighteen-man detachment rendezvoused with the cowhands at Horsehead, [48] which, in a scout five months earlier, he had found to be about three and one-half feet deep.[49]

Although the Comanche-Kiowa threat was over by 1875, Apaches still prowled the crossing, preying on travelers and the first cattlemen to graze cattle along the adjacent stretch of river. On December 17, 1877, Apaches stole seven or eight horses from Rooney's Ranch well upstream from Horsehead,[50] and two days later, fourteen Indians—likely the same band—struck a cow camp at the ford. Swooping down by morning, they escaped with fourteen horses and set the cowboys afoot. Unintimidated, three cowhands trailed the Indians to Castle Gap, where, in a fierce skirmish, they recaptured ten horses only to lose them again. With a wound felling one cowboy and the two able-bodied hands outnumbered seven to one, the three could only retreat to the Pecos.[51]

In October 1878, Second Lieutenant C. Esterly and a Fort Stockton detachment found the cow camps just above Horsehead abandoned,[52] presumably because of the Indian menace and the unyielding Pecos. However, by April 23, 1879, when Colonel George A. Armes of Fort Stockton crossed Horsehead and marched to Castle Gap, ranchers again dared the river. "The cowboys," Armes observed in his diary that evening, "are very glad to see us looking out for their protection and [are] much encouraged."

Two months later on June 18, Armes learned by messenger late in the day that Indians had been sighted at Horsehead. "I at once saddled up and ordered the command in a gallop, following the trail for twenty miles with fifteen cowboys who joined my command," he wrote, "but the Indians have scattered into the mountains, and it is impossible to find them."

Nevertheless, Armes marched his party on into the night and did not end the pursuit until they reached Castle Gap, sixty miles from his previous camp.[53]

On August 20 of that year, a Sergeant Briscoe of Fort Stockton and ten enlisted men, on reaching a cow camp at Horsehead, learned that Indians had stolen eight horses. The sergeant, eight soldiers, and three cowboys picked up the trail three miles downstream and took up the chase. Ten miles down the trail, at a camp only recently vacated, they recovered two horses stolen from the Richards Ranch above the ford, as well as four horses, a bridle, and two blankets from the Horsehead operation.

Marching northward, the men picked up the trail again in mid-afternoon and halted at dark after enduring sixty-five miles in the saddle that day. At daybreak they veered east with the trail to discover, just after midday, a horse slain for its meat. After another nine miles to the north, they found their own horses weakening and a strange country ahead, forcing them to abandon the chase.[54]

The same year, eighteen-year-old trail boss J. D. Jackson, pointing a herd west into the desert from the Middle Concho, disregarded the tried-and-proven method of driving day and night to reach the Pecos and water. Although the older hands resisted, Jackson drove only by dark and rested the beeves in daytime. Successfully gaining Horsehead, Jackson also improvised a novel way to cope with the inevitable stampede into the river. Taking the lead, he splashed his horse across to a sandbar in mid-river and stayed half the night, letting the cattle drink but keeping them from drifting downstream where the steepening banks would imprison them.[55]

Although the next few years brought the end of Indian depredations on the Pecos, Horsehead's reputation for violence grew worse, due to outlaws and lawlessness. For example, in the early 1880s, the crossing proved the focal point of a days-long chase that ended with a rifle shot and a lonely grave.

Drifter Tom Green, apparently hiring on with the U Ranch eleven miles northwest of present Sterling City, soon grew infatuated with the teen-age daughter of cowboy John Manning, whose cabin lay on the North Concho River near ranch headquarters. Discovering his daughter and Green missing one morning, Manning seized his buffalo gun and, with several other men, took up the trail of a wagon bearing south. Although the girl may have gone willingly at first (she had taken her clothes), shreds of a dress dotting the ruts suggested that she had reneged and begun marking the route for pursuers.

The trail led the men by the Foster Ranch on Sterling Creek and west to Horsehead Crossing. Fording the river and sighting the wagon ahead, Manning implored his companions to stay behind and let him administer frontier justice. Riding on alone, Manning killed Green with his buffalo gun and rescued the girl, who was bound

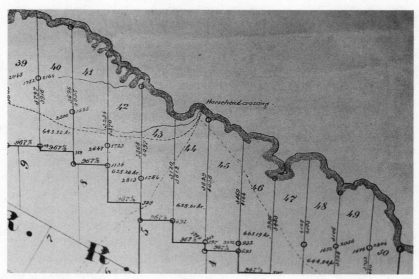

An 1890 Pecos County survey map pinpointing Horsehead Crossing. (courtesy, Clayton Wheat Williams Collection, N. S. Haley Memorial Library, Midland, Texas)

securely in the wagon. Soon thereafter, someone reported the killing to a Horsehead cattle outfit, and Hez Ray and other cowhands rode out and buried Green on the spot.[56]

"No court was ever troubled to make an inquiry into the matter . . ," related newspaperman W. F. Kellis, who settled in the North Concho valley in 1887. "[Killing] was the customary way of settling such things then. In those days it was extremely dangerous to fool with an old man's young girl in that way. . . . If a young fellow wanted his girl, he always asked for her. Otherwise he flirted with the gravediggers."[57]

A horse wrangler with an 1894 cattle drive tempted his own gravediggers in the chill of a blizzard at Horsehead. En route from a Davis Mountains ranch northeastward to the Panhandle, the man and nine other hands reached the crossing's west bank on a February afternoon and decided to hold the herd until morning. Compelled to guard the horses in the bitter cold of night, the wrangler built a life-sustaining fire with brush from a rat's den, only to fall asleep and let the animals wander. Awakening, he set off in search and became lost in the bends of the river. At one o'clock the next afternoon, his fellow hands finally found him—twelve miles upstream.[58]

On into the twentieth century, Horsehead continued to ply its treachery. In 1901, twenty-two-year-old Erving McElroy and another cowhand set out from the John T. McElroy "lower ranch" for Horsehead, thirty miles southwest, and a roundup near Fort Stockton.

"Each one of us had six horses and a roll of bedding tied on one," recalled Erving McElroy in 1972.

> We got to the river . . . and it was bank full. . . . The man I was with looked at me . . . and he says, "Are you afraid?" "Why," I says, "no. I was raised on the Mississippi . . . . I can pretty near run and jump that." So we plunged off into the river. Well, his horse got across and hit the bank. And just about that time, my horse turned around and started back—I knew I wasn't going to go back, 'cause the [river] . . .made another bend that made the water run fast. I knew I couldn't make it 'cause the banks was straight up and down. So I just slid off and, when I went down, I thought I never would come up. I had a pair of boots on, pair of spurs, and it was hard swimming. But I'd swum a long ways in the Mississippi

River and thought I was a good swimmer.

The other cowhand, seeing McElroy's plight, fought to control his own bolting horse and turn it to the river. Continued McElroy:

> He had a hard time to get his rope off the horn of the saddle when he saw me struggling in the stream. But he got his rope off and he throwed his loop out there to me. . . . I just throwed my arm over in there and drawed the rope to my body. And when he went to pulling on the rope, I went under, but . . . after I struck the bottom, [he] drug me on out and I was all right.[59]

The fencing of the open range rendered the full Goodnight-Loving Trail impractical soon after 1910, but on regional drives cowboys pushed beeves and horses across Horsehead for another two decades. As a young man, Russell Dyer (who was born in 1896) crossed beeves at the ford several times in taking herds from Terrell County to Odessa. Each drive required a horse wrangler, a cook, and eight or ten drovers whose stiffest test came at Horsehead.

"As I remember, it was pretty solid [on bottom] . . . and the chuck wagon, the mules, would go on across . . . ," Dyer noted in 1968. "Several times we had to swim the cattle across and we'd float the chuck wagon—the river would be up. . . . We'd tie our ropes onto the wagon, the tongue, and help the cook get across."[60]

In late December 1917, Sam Brown and Bill Tucker, fighting devastating drought on Brown's ranch twenty-five miles southeast of Midland, sent Dewitt "Shag" Ethridge and twenty-year-old Tyson Midkiff southwest to the Pecos with thirty to forty horses.

"They were starving to death where they were," recalled Midkiff more than seven decades later. "We took the horses over there and delivered them to Ted Brown and another boy at Horsehead Crossing. They had some country leased on the other side. I think it took us about four and a half days."

In making the drive, the men stayed overnight at the C. C. Johnson Ranch (about twenty miles south of Midland), the Jones Ranch, the McElroy or Y Ranch, and the Bill Cowden spread near present Crane. Said Midkiff:

We just turned the horses loose [each night]. If there was a water trough some place, they wouldn't go very far. We didn't have any wagon—we didn't even have anything tied on the saddle to eat. I remember Bill Tucker brought us a New Year's Day [1918] dinner and we eat it out in the pasture at the Ys. That's the first time I'd ever been to Horsehead Crossing, [so when] we got to Cowden's Ranch, [George Cowden] told us how to get across to there. We followed by directions and just old wagon roads.

At noon on the fifth day, Midkiff and Ethridge reached Horsehead to turn the horses into the river.

It was a wide stretch [of bank] you could cross—a hundred yards maybe. There wasn't any brush, [and] there weren't any steep banks there. I rode my horse across it, and we met them boys there on the other side. We turned the horses over to them. It was about forty or fifty feet across it, [and] if the river got up, the water would first rise on the other [west] side 'cause it was low. It hadn't rained in a long time; I don't think the river was much over a foot, foot and a half deep. It was an easy crossing.[61]

With mile-wide floods sometimes roaring down the Pecos, Horsehead, like other fords, constantly evolved. In 1919 or 1920, cowhand Walter Boren (who was born in 1900) found no sign of the once-dreaded quicksands. "The river run . . . knee-deep . . . over a bunch of flat rock," he recalled in 1990.[62] By 1924, when twenty-four-year-old cowboy Gid Reding reined his horse into the water, even the exact points of passage known to nineteenth-century travelers had vanished into legend.

"Where I crossed was a rock bottom," recalled Reding in 1989. "[But] I think the crossing was wherever the last big flood . . . left a place. . . . That river would get up a month at a time."[63]

Ranching's pre-mechanization era saw its last reported crossings of herds at Horsehead in 1928. Chon Villalba, born in 1900, recalled in 1990 that he and four other Scharbauer Ranch cowboys crossed Hereford cattle back and forth at the site on three occasions in week-long drives between Scharbauer holdings at Midland and southeast of Fort Stockton.

"It looked like a ditch," said Villalba, who added that the chuck wagon crossed on a bridge downstream near Girvin. "[It] didn't have much water when we went through—it might hit to the belly of the horses."[64]

Although herds as large as 12,000 head once had watered at Horsehead during the peak years of the Goodnight-Loving Trail, [65] none of the 1928 Scharbauer herds exceeded 100 beeves, noted Villalba.[66]

By the 1930s, Horsehead's fate was sealed and even its 1928 location was veiled in mystery. To the distant rumble of automobiles headed for bridges, terrific floods washed away virtually all signs of the crossing, while brush and swirls of sand choked the wagon ruts. Nature and technology had worked together to close a chapter in American history, never to reopen it.[67] Even so, Horsehead Crossing still stands as a monument to the fortitude of those who pioneered the western frontier. ★

Tyson Midkiff in 1989. (author)

Chon Villalba in 1990. (author)

Below a great rock that marked a ford and served as a lookout against Apaches, the Pecos rushes through a jumble of boulders laid by pioneer hand.

Little is left today of so-called Spanish Dam, situated in obscurity seven miles south of present McCamey. But even before the impounded water first sent a current sluicing through an ambitious, fifteen-mile-long canal in the 1870s, the site loomed important for peaceful Indians and, perhaps, for Spanish explorers.

The Great Rock, an isolated limestone mass seventy feet high, seven hundred feet long, and varying from one hundred to three hundred feet wide, rises suddenly out of a plain to front the Pecos. This upthrust, lying just north and east of the river, is unique in a land where a pioneer could have journeyed for days upstream without finding more than a knoll guarding the river's bare banks.

A mortar hole on the slope of the Great Rock. (author)

Situated on a fringe of the Chihuahuan Desert, the Great Rock and its immediate surroundings afforded peaceful Indians of the seventeenth century several advantages. Elsewhere, the Pecos coursed swift and turbid between sheer banks plagued by quicksand, but here the life-giving waters, teeming with fish, turtles, and mussels, flowed over a gravelly bed between sloping banks that allowed easy fording. Too, the hundred-yard-wide flat between the river and bluff was suitable not only for campfires and tule huts but also for fields of corn, beans, and pumpkins. The rocky bluff, meanwhile, proved ideal for mortar holes and sunken ovens known as mescal pits.

Considering the Apache threat of the seventeenth century, however, the Great Rock's utmost advantage may have been a tactical one. From its summit, a sentry could have spotted a raiding party (as well as buffalo or deer) several miles across a wasteland bearing only scrub mesquite and creosote. And in an actual attack, the steep escarpment would have been easy to defend from the dome above, where the remnants of fortifications still were evident in the twentieth century.[1]

"Up on this little hill there, they've got some holes and rocks so they could guard it, you know, put up battle," noted Cliff Newland (1886-1979), who studied the site after going to work for the McElroy Ranch in neighboring Upton County in 1928.[2]

It was such a rancheria bustling with activity that the Spaniard Juan Dominguez de Mendoza and his party approached in January 1684. With soldiers, Roman Catholic missionaries, and Indian guides and servants, Mendoza had set out from present El Paso in mid-December 1683 to confer in central Texas with representatives of nineteen Indian "nations."[3]

They struck the Salado, or Pecos, on January 13, somewhere between modern Imperial and Girvin, and forged downstream on the southwest side. On January 17, as they crossed land charred by fire, Mendoza sighted what he described as a "great rock" ahead.[4] Although historian J. W. Williams believed this topographic feature to be the 365-foot prominence near S Crossing and the present Texas Highway 349 river bridge, authorities such as O. W. Williams and Victor J. Smith identified the "great rock" with the later site of Spanish Dam.[5]

Halting within a league (2.63 miles) of the bluff, Mendoza found a contingent of Jediondo Indians approaching. Although most were on foot, a few rode horses—an indication of how early the tribes of the Pecos assimilated this foreign animal into their cultures.

Too, the Jediondos evidently were no strangers to Spaniards and Roman Catholicism. Not only did they greet Mendoza's party with rejoicing and a salutatory volley of gunfire, but they carried a large wooden cross, painted red and yellow, and a white banner with two crosses of blue taffeta.

Nevertheless, Mendoza took precautions against attack, and allowed only two priests to dismount. When the Jediondos merely kissed the priests' garments, Mendoza and his party followed them to their rancheria, which he described in his report as lying "at the foot of a great rock that serves it as protection against the hostile Apaches."

Crossing the Pecos to the middle of the village, the expedition encountered further jubilation, this time on the part of the women and children. Despite the outwardly warm welcome, Mendoza declined an invitation for lodging and entertainment in the rancheria "because of the evil results which might follow." On a nearby hill—chosen, he said, "according to the usage of war"—he camped seven days while "awaiting news of a great ambuscade which the enemy [the Apaches] are coming to make on them [the Jediondos] in order to carry off many horses."[6]

Despite the Spanish encampment, possibly in the Bobcat Hills a couple of miles to the north,[7] Apaches swooped down by night and, from the very shadow of the Great Rock, drove away an unspecified number of Jediondo horses. The fear of such raids, which claimed more horses than human lives, prompted the Jediondo and Jumano chiefs to petition Mendoza on January 19 to "make war on the hostile Apaches, who were enemies of theirs and of the Spaniards." Mendoza, aware of the Apache threat to Spanish interests, consented.[8]

Spain was powerful and determined, but in the desert the Apaches had few equals. Two centuries after Mendoza's promise of warfare, Spanish occupation of Texas was only a dim memory—and Apaches still swooped in by dark to spill blood and steal horses below the Great Rock.

Provided deerskins by the Jediondos so that his soldiers "might be armed" in the war against the Apaches, Mendoza soon forged eastward to disappear into history, and the Jediondos, too, faded into oblivion.[9]

By the mid-1870s emigrant wagon trains, cattle herds, and stagecoaches were raising dust over the Pecos, and a settlement was burgeoning near the army post of Fort Stockton, thirty-seven miles west-southwest of the Great Rock. The days of the dreaded Comanche war trail had just ended, and, though at times Apache raiders still jumped the reservation near present Ruidoso, New Mexico, four men looked to the Great Rock and envisioned a remarkable farming project along what one newspaper correspondent considered an ideal river for irrigation.

"It is estimated that the Pecos contains a larger supply of water for purposes of irrigation than the Rio Grande at El Paso . . . ," said "H. C. K." in the May 25, 1877, *San Antonio Daily Express*. "[Its valley] is readily irrigable. The soil is a deep yellow loam, very loose."[10]

Prodded by the Texas Legislature's 1875 act "to encourage the construction of canals and ditches for navigation and irrigation,"[11] Cesario Torres, Bernardo Torres, Juan Torres, and Felis Garza organized the Torres Irrigation and Manufacturing Company by May

The remnants of Spanish Dam today. (author)

20 of that year. For each mile of irrigation canal they completed, the state would grant them four or more sections of adjoining land, assuming the waterway attained at least three miles in length.[12]

Cesario Torres, a Pecos County justice of the peace, was born in Mexico in 1834 and immigrated to San Antonio with his family at age three. As an adult, he rose to prominence in San Antonio before venturing west to Fort Stockton. In 1869 and 1870, Torres and his brother Bernardo helped Garza construct a one-and-a-half-mile-long irrigation ditch from Comanche Springs to their three separate 160-acre farms.[13]

With the 1875 act, the Torres company's plan was to impound water at the Great Rock and channel it along the southwest side of the river more than fourteen miles downstream to Pontoon Bridge—the important crossing on the Upper Road—and Horseshoe Bend beyond.[14] To do so would require the construction of a rock dam, probably the first such structure to challenge the Texas stretch of this flood-prone river.

With crowbar, sledgehammer, and pioneer determination, the Torres company freed the loose limestone shielding the Great Rock, and, at a point in the river opposite the hill's lower end, dumped wagonload after wagonload into a frame of logs (possibly cypress) imported from afar. Then the company set about quarrying and blasting the Great Rock's west face; even today, the bluff carries linear marks where laborers drove spikes into the limestone.[15]

In all, "between three and four thousand wagon loads" splashed into the Pecos, according to the May 25, 1877, *San Antonio Daily Express*, whose correspondent marveled at this feat of "primitive engineering backed by perseverance." Never a dam in the classic sense, it nevertheless impeded the current sufficiently to raise the water level for two hundred yards upstream, where a canal nine feet wide intersected the river.[16]

"It made a waterfall," said Billy Rankin, who was first at the site as an eighteen-year-old in 1924. "You'd never think of it being a dam. . . . [They] just slid those rocks down and built it up there."[17]

"There's rock there that weighed, I'll bet, four or five tons," Cliff Newland recalled in 1964. "How they ever got them out in the Pecos River—quarried them off and got them down there a quarter of a mile—I don't know."[18]

With irrigation water now diverted fifteen miles downstream through the bordering flats, the Torres company and its labor force of fifty Mexican families soon had in cultivation five hundred acres of wheat, corn, barley, beans, and other crops.

"These crops are reported as now promising an unusually heavy yield," reported the *San Antonio Express* in 1877.[19]

Headquarters, situated eight miles downstream of the dam, [20] consisted of a fifty-by-eighty-foot adobe house and fifteen primitive residences or barns, some constructed of pinion pine daubed with mud. Originating in the forests of New Mexico, the timbers had come down the Pecos in the form of rafts guided by trappers returning from beaver country.[21]

Even as the Torres operation grew to eight hundred acres,[22] the Apache threat persisted, just as it had for the Jediondos two centuries before.

On April 22, 1877, Indians galloped their mounts through the fields of the Torres farm and made off with five horses. Seven days later, a second attack brought the loss of another nine horses and mules, as well as the herd of work animals.[23] In early May, a *San Antonio Express* correspondent arrived by stage at Pontoon Bridge, near the south end of the irrigation canal, to learn that Indians had stolen the Torres farm's entire remuda of horses and mules the night before.[24]

It was inevitable that the situation would spawn bloodshed. In the summer of 1877, five Indians ambushed Pecos County surveyor Thomas C. Nelson at a point of rocks twenty to thirty miles downstream from Torres headquarters. One slug exploded into his left breast, while a second sailed through his hat and a third punctured his canteen and embedded in his saddle. Nelson fought back, killing or wounding an Indian before escaping on horseback. He made a desperate, bloody ride for help to the Torres farm, where, even two weeks later, he remained in serious condition. He returned to the county seat at Fort Stockton in mid-August, a month in which several parties, including Cesario Torres, unsuccessfully took up the trail of the marauders.[25]

From its inception, the Torres farm relied heavily on emigrant and U.S. Army wagon trains as a market for its produce; the Lower and Upper roads merged just downstream near Pontoon Bridge and skirted the Torres headquarters. But with the completion of the Texas & Pacific Railroad across West Texas in 1881, fewer wagoners traveled the route, forcing the Torres group to close the operation and sell most of the holdings to rancher Eugene

McCrowen. However, when fellow rancher Andrew Young of Coleman County acquired the property from McCrowen in 1883, one member of the Torres clan still lived and farmed along the canal, according to Young's son, Arthur, who was a boy at the time.

Gaining control of ten miles of riverfront for his free-ranging cattle and horses, the elder Young established his headquarters along the flowing ditch.[26] However, with September 1884 rains swelling portions of the Pecos to a reported three miles wide,[27] treacherous currents breached the dam.[28] Still, much of the structure would remain intact for more than four decades.[29]

On January 12, 1883, a silver spike joined two lines of track three miles west of the Pecos-Rio Grande confluence and opened up the transcontinental Southern Pacific Railroad.[30] The presence of the SP bridge at the mouth of the Pecos, and the T&P bridge far upstream at Barstow, plunged Pontoon Bridge into neglect and disrepair. And two hundred years after Mendoza's passing, wagoners and horsemen looked again to the ford guarded by the Great Rock for relatively safe passage. On into the 1920s, the "Old Rock Dam Crossing" endured as a preferred crossing point.

Fort Stockton resident O. W. Williams, writing in 1902, noted that, of the three wagon crossings in the area, "[the ford] known as the Torres Dam crossing, at the site of a great rock on the east, was the best and safest. It was the least subject to overflowed banks and its bottom was smooth and hard."[31]

In 1907, ten-year-old Tyson Midkiff and his family, traveling by covered wagon from Midland County southwest to Fort Stockton, halted on the bank of the ford.

"Where that dam was falling over there, why, we camped there, just about noon and caught some fish, big ol' blue catfish," said Midkiff in an 1991 interview. "Most of the banks were right straight up and down, but down there where the wagon sort of circled, you could see where the wagon road went across it. It was . . . maybe a hundred yards [downstream] from where that water was falling over. That water was roaring; it made a waterfall."

Upon easing the wagon down into the crossing, Midkiff's grandfather took measures to guard the safety of the woman and seven children riding with him. Recalled Midkiff, "The horses had their feet on the bottom, [but] the water was up pretty near to the wagon bed. And my granddaddy, he got right out on the double tree there and kept the horses going. Wanted to be sure they didn't stop the wagon in the water, 'cause it was moving on pretty good, you know."[32]

In 1924, Billy Rankin, a cowboy with the White and Baker Ranch Company, crossed the Pecos at the Great Rock on two occasions during a six-week span.

Billy Rankin in 1982. (author)

"We brought a chuck wagon over from the old [ranch] headquarters, and we crossed on the dam," recalled Rankin, who said the rocks had a crest width of ten to fifteen feet. "The water was about [eighteen inches] high over the top of them; it wasn't up in the wagon bed. And then I came back across it thirty or forty days later, just bringing a pack horse across it. It didn't get my bed wet or nothing like that."[33]

Sometime during the next few years, flood waters further breached the dam at the northeast end, spelling its doom. Too, as the level of the Pecos dropped with the construction of modern dams far upstream, boulders lining the exposed banks were hauled away for use elsewhere.[34]

But as the limestone boulders yielded to nature and man, the Great Rock from which they had come continued steadfast, sheltering, perhaps, the secret of a lost treasure. Cliff Newland, who hunted for the treasures of the Pecos country for half a lifetime, believed the hill to be the site of "one of the biggest dat-gum Spanish camps you'll find"—and possibly a Spanish cache as well.[35] In 1902, O. W. Williams reported that the "fancied deposit" was Mexican silver and that twenty years after the end of the Torres farming operation, American fortune hunters had "pitted and scarred" the dome in search of it.[36]

The Great Rock is not alone among hills of the area in shielding legendary treasure. Three miles south of the old Torres headquarters and just west of Big Harkey Canyon in Pecos County, a sudden-walled spur of 3,100-foot-high Indian Mesa cradles a hollow forty to fifty feet in diameter and six to twenty feet deep. In 1883, Arthur Young came to know it as the "Old Mine," the site of Spanish diggings. Lending credence to the tale was a ravine—the possible remnant of a road—leading from the depression to the Pecos, less than three miles away.[37]

Roy McDonald, born in 1906 and raised nearby, had reason to accept the account.

"When I was a kid, you could still [see] that old hole up under that mesa," he related. "The native Indians in this country used to get silver out of there some. Later on, the Spaniards found out about it, and they moved in there and mined nearly all of that silver. I remember when I was a kid we used to go over there and find nuggets laying around there that was real heavy, had silver in them. But they say you go over there now and there's been so many people in there, you can't even find any rock there."[38]

The tale always has had its skeptics.

"It's on my ranch, [and] people have come up with all kinds of ideas—from a mine to a meteor hitting it—of which none, in my opinion, are true," said William B. Wilson, who, in 1945, took up White and Baker land comprising the site. "[Big] Harkey Canyon's a real steep canyon, very scenic canyon, [and] as you come out of that canyon going north toward the Pecos River, to the west there's a series of fault lines. You can see the face of that cliff where the two sides have rubbed together. If you'll go from that sinkhole—as we call it—in a northwesterly direction, there's a series of other sinkholes, but they're not as big as this one. I don't think it ever was a mine."[39]

"They called it the Old Spanish Mine," acknowledged Billy Rankin, who learned of it while cowboying at its rim for White and Baker in 1923. "Personally, I don't think there was enough silver ever taken out of that thing to have made a silver filling for a small tooth."[40]

Like that mysterious mesa and its mine of fact or fancy, the Great Rock remains secretive even to this day, but the remnant boulders of Spanish Dam do not. In the sudden, brief rapids they spawn, they still proclaim loudly the initiative and ingenuity of nineteenth-century pioneers. ★

The so-called Old Spanish Mine below Indian Mesa. (author)

★ *Chapter 6*
Pontoon Crossing

On its water-logged planks, East met West for eleven crucial years in the 1870s and 1880s.

Floating on the Pecos ten miles northwest of present Iraan, Pontoon Bridge, built in 1870, immediately became the most important crossing point ever known on this treacherous river. Twice by the late 1860s, authorities had bridged the river downstream near Fort Lancaster, but it had refused to be tamed, its sudden floods sweeping away the crude structures. The river rushed unyielding on into the 1870s, when travelers finally gained an enduring reprieve with the Pontoon Bridge, which did not avoid the Pecos as much as become a part of it.

By the late 1860s, travelers could cross the Texas stretch of the Pecos only at widely spaced intervals, and the most frequently used ford—Horsehead Crossing—was fraught with danger of Indian attack.

In the search for a safer crossing and shorter Upper Road route between Fort Concho (at present San Angelo) on the east and Fort Stockton on the west,[1] Captain F. S. Dodge of the latter fort scouted the Pecos well below Horsehead in May 1868. Despite a reported crossing north-northeast of present Bakersfield, Dodge found only unyielding river. Still faced with fording in order to blaze a wagon route northeast to the Middle Concho River and existing Concho-Stockton road, Dodge finally gained difficult passage far downstream at the Riffles below present Iraan.

"From the . . . trails found here, I am of the opinion that this must be the regular crossing of the Indians on route from the northern plains to Mexico and back to the plains . . . ," he reported. "I found a good crossing for horses but am of the opinion that dismounted men could not ford it on account of the swiftness of the current."[2]

Despite the failure to find a suitable natural ford, Colonel Edward Hatch on July 1, 1868, ordered the mail line changed from the Horsehead route to the southerly course trekked by Dodge. In order to surmount the Pecos barrier, Hatch charged Fort Stockton's commander with engineering a crossing.[3]

Dodge, failing again two weeks later to find a ford along the route, turned his command into the river northeast of modern Bakersfield at Pecos Mail Station, a west-bank stage stand situated a short distance downstream of the point where the Lower Road from San Antonio veered west from the Pecos.

"I crossed the Pecos at this point [on July 15], swimming my horses and crossing the men, arms, ammunition, etc. on a raft made of a wagon bed and barrels . . . ," he wrote. "There is no ford that I could find at the Pecos Mail Station that light vehicles and horses can be crossed easily."

Dodge added an important observation: "The stream being quite narrow at this point, [it] could be bridged with little difficulty."[4]

The search for a new crossing soon led the U.S. Army to a location three and one-half road miles below Pecos Mail Station. There, where a gap opened up between hills guarding the east bank, authorities identified a site and set to work.[5] They could do nothing about the rapid current, but the sharp banks were another matter. On August 31, Lieutenant Robert Neely and Company A, Forty-first Infantry, received orders to "encamp where the new road leaves the Pecos . . . [and] dig down the banks of the river and make the crossing as convenient as possible."[6] Nevertheless, the ford proved formidable.

"There is no sign of a river . . . no banks, trees, 'nor nothing,'" wrote H. C. Logan, who rode a westbound stage to the site in the fall of 1868. "The result is, before you know it you are in it. It is a deep, turbid stream, very swift, very crooked, quite narrow—not more than thirty feet wide—and the muddiest stream I ever saw; the banks on both sides are about three feet high."

From the start, authorities realized a ferry was essential.

"Coaches [are] being kept on both sides," Logan noted. "The

crossing . . . causes some delay, a canoe being used to ferry over the mail and passengers."[7]

To guard the new mail route, a detail from Fort Stockton, in July 1868, occupied Camp Melvin (or Melbourne) approximately one mile downstream on the river's east bank.[8] Situated about three

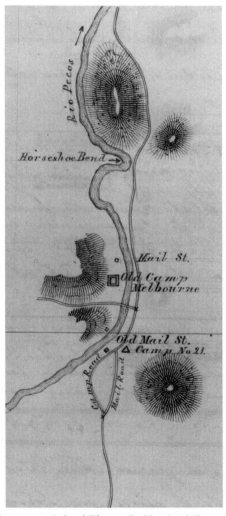

Brevet Lieutenant Colonel Thomas B. Hunt's 1869 map of Camp Melbourne (Melvin) and the mail crossing. (National Archives)

miles northwest of the present Texas Highway 349 bridge over the Pecos, the camp may have existed prior to the rerouting of the stage line, for Brevet Lieutenant Colonel Thomas B. Hunt referred to it in 1869 as an "old Camp."[9] It consisted of a 120-foot-by-189.5-foot rock corral (with 18-inch-thick walls), and a 50-foot-by-68-foot stone building (with a 12-foot-by-12-foot addition on the southeast) that may have included a guardhouse mentioned in U.S. Army records.[10]

Because the Pecos often was too briny for human consumption, Camp Melvin's troops evidently transported drinking water from a hand-dug well a short distance eastward up the stage road.

"It was about two miles north of the river," noted Paul Patterson, who first traveled to the site by wagon in the mid-1920s. "We'd stop there and camp. The water wasn't very good to drink, [but] you *could* drink it. . . . They called it Government Well."[11]

"It's right on the [Texas 349] highway almost," said Tom Vandevanter, whose ranch of the 1990s included the well and Camp Melvin. "I put casing in it [in the mid-1960s] and built it up, graveled it and sealed it over, and we're still using it."[12]

From the summer of 1868 on, Camp Melvin occupied a unique position in westward travel, for the two major routes across West Texas—the Lower and Upper roads—converged a short distance across the river from its walls.

"Camp Melvin . . . ," wrote paymaster Major C. M. Tunnel in 1869, "was no doubt adopted as the stage crossing in the hopes that the Lancaster Bridge [which then spanned the river about thirty-two road miles downstream] could be moved up to that point and made available for both roads."[13]

Fort Stockton's commander, Captain George Gamble, made just such an attempt upon the receipt of orders dated November 23, 1868.

"I had the bridge taken up immediately . . . ," he reported on December 8. "But as the river at the mail crossing [Camp Melvin] is too wide to put the present bridge across at any point within three or four miles, I ordered the post quartermaster to replace it at the same point as before near Lancaster.

"It will require a bridge at least sixty-five feet long to span the river at the mail crossing, and it will cost, including lumber, iron, and expense of building, $10,000, it being necessary to bring the lumber from the pinery above Fort Davis, being a distance of one hundred seventy miles."

Ironically, Gamble added his conviction that such a structure was unessential along a route that he believed the military and public would neglect.

"I do not think it necessary to have a bridge at the mail crossing, simply for the accommodation of a few pounds of mail three times a week," he said. "It was customary when contractors ran the mail over this route before the war, for them to build flat boats for crossing at all these streams. Mr. [Ben] Ficklin [of the stage line] might provide one at this point that would only cost a few hundred dollars."[14]

Despite Gamble's prediction, westbound wagons soon creaked one after another along the new road to Camp Melvin, en route to Fort Stockton—fifty-five miles west—and beyond. On May 1, 1869, young Harriet Bunyard bid adieu to Collin County, Texas, and set out for California in an eleven-wagon caravan carrying eight families with twenty men.[15] On June 15, only two days ahead of a trailing wagon train, the emigrants reached the Pecos at Camp Melvin, whose picket had been reduced to eight men with the March removal of two Fort Stockton cavalry companies to Fort Concho.[16]

"The Pecos is a narrow, deep, and muddy stream with no timber on its banks," Harriet wrote in her diary. "It is now level with the banks. Very bad tast[ing] water."

Gaining permission to ferry belongings across in the mail skiff, the emigrants fought the Pecos the entire day of the sixteenth.

"They . . . tied ropes to the wagons and crossed," wrote Harriet. "One wagon came uncoupled in the river. Another broke the rope that was on the tongue, but those on the opposite side still had hold of the other ropes and the men swam in and brought all safe to shore."

By 3:00 p.m., all the wagons and contents had gained the west bank. Still, there remained the cattle and horses to force into the muddy flow.

"They kept crossing until about ten o'clock in the night," recorded Harriet. "When anything would start down stream they would plunge in and bring them out. It is only a few places that the stock can get down to the water without going in overhead."

Although only a single mule drowned in the operation, the Pecos came close to wreaking worse tragedy.

"Just about the time all the wagons were over, brother Dan [Bunyard] and Ed Stewart with several others jumped into the river to try their speed swimming," wrote Harriet. "The current being very swift, Ed Stewart cramped and was sinking the last time when they caught him. In trying to rescue Ed, Dan came very near drowning, being so near exhausted. The skiff was pushed to them and they got in and came safe to land. How we all were frightened, but luck[y] for us, all came safe."

Finally resuming her westward journey the next afternoon, Harriet was not sorry to see the Pecos peril recede.

"The men have labored faithful in getting across the river that has so much been dreaded," she wrote. "All is over safe now, and I am truly thankful. . . . While we were loading, the train that was behind came to the opposite bank. I can sympathize with them, for I know that they dread crossing this stream."[17]

Such trials led the U.S. Army to study the site for a potential bridge only four months later, when Major C. M. Tunnel found the river 40.6 to 53.6 feet wide at or near the ferry.[18] "I think a crossing can easily be found of from forty-one to forty-six feet almost anywhere above Camp Melvin within a distance of ten miles," he observed. "A bridge fifty feet in length would be ample."

As a U.S. Army paymaster, Tunnel believed that financial considerations demanded that such a bridge straddle the Pecos seven to ten miles north of Camp Melvin on a direct Concho-to-Stockton

A remnant wall at Camp Melvin. (author)

line. "It would shorten the road from Austin or San Antonio to Fort Stockton enough to pay for the bridge in a short time by the savings in mileage on the transportation of supplies to Stockton and above," he wrote.[19]

While Lieutenant Colonel C. Grover, on January 23, also favored a site upstream of Melvin,[20] he noted that many points along the river were ideal.

"The banks of the Pecos are of such a character," he said, "that no difficulty will be had in finding a suitable place for a bridge sixty feet or less long." Recommending that Fort Stockton quartermaster J. L. Humfreville oversee construction, Grover noted that "if the bridge is built in the pineries above Fort Davis, and hauled to the river by government transportation, it will cost . . . from thirteen to fifteen hundred ($1,500), transportation not considered."[21]

Despite the arguments for placing the structure elsewhere, during the first few months of 1870 a bridge spanned the Pecos immediately adjacent to Camp Melvin's main building and stage station.[22] Evidently owned jointly by the government and Ben Ficklin's San Antonio and El Paso Mail line,[23] the structure was "an ingenious piece of work . . . ," wrote O. W. Williams, who crossed on April 12, 1880. "A pontoon swung by iron chains between banks, [it had] movable platforms on either side as approaches to the pontoon, to fit any stage of the water."[24]

In designing the structure, Humfreville also had to take into account a disparity in the opposing banks. "The animals can be watered on the left [northeast] bank," Second Lieutenant Thomas C. Davenport noted in his February 7, 1874 scout to Pontoon, "but not on the right on account of the height."[25]

Although the bridge, supported by pontoons or boats resting on the water and anchored to the banks, was strong enough to accommodate ordinary wagon or stage travel, it could not support heavily loaded prairie schooners. "Consequently I was compelled to divide my freight, which consisted mostly of copper, and had to carry each lot over separately," wrote freighter August Santleben of his return trip from Chihuahua, Mexico, in 1872. "The laborious undertaking consumed almost the entire day."[26]

With passing wagoners creating a market for agricultural produce, Cesario Torres and his relatives undertook a farming project adjacent to the bridge in 1870. The tenant farmers, who were Mexican, irrigated from the Pecos and lived primitively. "They seemed to be real poor—living in underground holes," noted the Fort Davis surgeon's report of June 2. "They use the ancient plow consisting of a long beam, at one end of which a pointed stick is secured at an acute angle."[27]

Among the travelers passing the farming operation was Emily K. Andrews, who accompanied her husband, Colonel George Lippitt Andrews, from Austin to his command at Fort Davis in 1874. The party, including their young daughter Maud and thirteen soldiers, reached the Pecos at Camp Melvin about 4:00 p.m. on August 24 and prepared to cross, which required forethought despite the bridge.

"The pontoon bridge over this river is not very safe, and if the water is high the teams have all to be unloaded, the baggage being carried over by hand," Emily wrote in her diary. "The mules being accustomed to fording the rivers are very unwilling to try the bridge, and we found it necessary to put a man at the head of each, before they would cross. Maud and I walked over as the mules were so frightened that the Col. thought it not quite safe for us to ride."

Making camp immediately across the structure, the party took refuge in their tents from a "driving Norther" and rain storm that brought a two-foot rise to the river. Nevertheless, the water level lay so far below the steep, western bank that the men had to water the mules and horses with buckets. Emily watched with amusement as her daughter's "little horse" Nellie sampled the muddy brine.

"Three of these [buckets] filled were standing in a row when it came Nellie's turn to drink," recorded Emily. "She put her nose to the first, then to the next and on to the third. By this time she was entirely disgusted and would have kicked them all over the bank if one of the men had not jumped to prevent it. Thirsty as she must have been, she would not touch a drop."[28]

Although the Indian presence at Horsehead Crossing had created the need for Pontoon Crossing, the bridge ironically lay in the midst of an enormous Indian camp from times past; charred rocks indicating old campfire rings were plentiful along the northeast bank.[29] Too, although avoiding Horsehead Crossing may have eased the minds of some travelers, it did not negate the Indian threat.

"The [mail] line from Fort Concho toward El Paso passes through the Llana or Stake[d] plains, generally known as the Sahara of the America," noted the *Texas Almanac* for 1870. "Entirely along this portion of the line the Comanches and Apaches, the most troublesome and bloodthirsty tribes of Indians, frequently commit severe depredations, not only to the mail line, but to the government trains and droves of cattle passing through the country. They frequently, by their skill (if it may be called such) stampede every hoof of stock belonging to a mail station, and . . . get possession of . . . mules belonging to a government train, thus leaving the train and wagoners at a complete stand-still . . . in a wild Indian country without wood or water."

In reporting the "great suffering" that Indian raids inflicted on wagoners, the almanac attributed most attacks to small war parties. "Still," added the writer, "the United States forces to watch them are much smaller, which the Indians are smart enough to know—hence the casualties."[30]

Although Brevet Lieutenant Colonel Thomas B. Hunt reported Camp Melvin "abandoned" in November 1869,[31] the Indian threat led pickets from Fort Stockton to frequent the outpost once Pontoon Bridge was in place. In May 1871, one sergeant and four privates were at Camp Melvin,[32] while by the following January authorities had reduced the guard to four.[33] Responding to an intensified threat by Apaches, one to three noncommissioned officers and four to nine privates—or the privates alone—served as station guards and stage escorts from January 1876 through October 1879.

Despite the military presence, hostiles haunted the Pontoon Crossing region just as they did other stretches of the Pecos.

On or about July 31, 1873, approximately thirteen Indians swooped down on the mail station at Melvin and killed Juan Chabarilla, who evidently herded the stage animals. The war party made off with twelve mules and two horses, all owned by the stage company.[35] Soon afterward near Horseshoe Bend, about two miles downstream on the Lower Road, Indians attacked Wilson Keith and his fellow drovers as they pushed six thousand beeves up the Pecos. Seriously wounded, Keith died after having his leg amputated in Seven Rivers, New Mexico.[36]

On June 2, 1874, a man named Torres (evidently Cesario Torres of the farming project) suffered a gunshot wound to the arm when fifteen Indians attacked his caravan near Camp Melvin and drove away approximately thirty-five horses and mules.[37] High water at Horsehead Crossing throughout the succeeding four weeks kept Fort Stockton troops from scouting to Castle Gap (twelve miles east-northeast of Horsehead) in search of the raiders.[38]

Although Ben Ficklin's mail company had lost only three mail shipments to Indians along its entire route through the 1860s,[39] stage drivers pushed their teams to Pontoon Bridge only at great peril in 1877 and 1878.

"It took a man with lots of nerve and strength to be a stage driver in the Indian days . . . ," noted onetime Texas Ranger James B. Gillett, who reached Pontoon with a Ranger detachment in 1879. "They were certainly the bravest of the brave."[40]

On October 22, 1877, attendants at Camp Melvin noted the failure of the westbound stage to rumble in on schedule. Despite a search by troops from Concho and Stockton, six days later the *San Antonio Daily Express* reported the vehicle still missing.[41] Finally, about sixteen miles northeast of Pontoon, a Fort Stockton patrol found traces of wagon ruts—and lone horse tracks—leaving the road. Riding south, troops came upon a grisly scene.

"About one hundred yards from the road was found the body of the driver [John Sanders] with one bullet hole in his body, which was stripped with the exception of the undershirt and one sock," reported Lieutenant Colonel M. M. Blunt, Fort Stockton's commander. "Also letters and papers and mail matter which had been carefully examined, letters being torn across and the pieces dropped, apparently in search of money. Bundles opened, contents taken and the wrappers left."

Less than half a mile away, the patrol discovered the abandoned stage and four sets of horse tracks leading south. Four miles on toward the Pecos, the patrol found where the path merged with a second trail, this one beaten by the hooves of eight or nine horses.

"The tracks of the hooves showed they were unshod," reported Blunt. "The tracks of the men [indicated] moccasins or buffalo shoes. All the horses and mail bags were carried off. The mail found was but a small portion of the whole."

With the trail days old and cold, the patrol soon gave up the chase, leaving the identities of the raiders a mystery. Blunt expressed his conviction that "all this was not done by Indians," and the *San Antonio Daily Express* reported that "the perpetrators of the murder and robbery were at least governed by white men, if they were not all white."[42]

On June 23, 1878, in Castle Gap, two cowboys charged an apparently lone Indian herding five horses. Suddenly, gunfire erupted from the nearby boulders, and before the echo died away in the

canyon, four concealed Indians had crippled a saddle horse and seriously wounded one cowhand. Second Lieutenant John Bigelow, Jr.,
and eight men scouted to the gap in search of the war party, but
failed to pick up the trail.[43]

Three days after the Castle Gap fight, five Indians afoot—
evidently the same war party—attacked the stage four to five miles
northeast of Pontoon Bridge and seriously wounded passenger Max
Schultz in the left thigh. A day later, on June 27, the stage reached
Fort Stockton and Schultz gained medical attention. The same
Indians, in all probability, also raided the nearby Torres farm and
shot Jose Garza in the leg.[44]

With three people wounded in separate attacks, likely by the
same war party, Captain D. D. Van Valzah of Fort Stockton, on June
28, dispatched Lieutenant W. H. Beck and twenty-five men with fifteen days' rations to track the hostiles.[45] Crossing Pontoon Bridge
and reaching the site of the stage attack, Beck learned that rain had
obliterated all signs except where the vehicle had swerved from the
road.

Scouting upstream on the river's west bank July 1 and 2,
Beck gained Horsehead Crossing, which he found "swimming full."

"There I met the man whose comrade had been shot at
Castle Gap Spring," he reported. "He swam the river and told me
that he and others had visited the spring since the skirmish, and that
the Indians had gone into the Sand Hills some days before."

Fruitless in his attempts to pick up the trail, Beck returned to
Fort Stockton on July 4.[46]

Because a pontoon bridge, by definition, was intended only
for temporary use, the structure at Camp Melvin demanded periodic
upkeep. On January 2, 1877, the superintendent of the Texas and
California Mail Company (as military records referred to it by then)
reported that the pontoon was rotten.[47] With no lumber available
near Fort Stockton, Captain Van Valzah contacted military headquarters in San Antonio on January 3 and requested four hundred
running feet of lumber in sections one and one-half inches thick and
sixteen feet long. He also ordered several gallons of tar, thirty pounds
of rosin, and thirty pounds of raw cotton.[48]

Despite the fact that ten months later one sergeant and two
privates spent six days effecting further restoration,[49] Lieutenant
Colonel Blunt of Fort Stockton reported on December 28 that "the
bridge is in very bad condition and requires considerable repairs."[50]

Obtaining the necessary lumber, two noncommissioned officers and
two to three privates labored from February 22 to March 5, 1878, to
mend the structure.[51] Nevertheless, less than four months later, on
June 28, Captain Van Valzah requested iron bolts and more lumber
for additional upkeep.[52] These repairs, performed July 8 to July 18,
required the services of one noncommissioned officer and four privates from Company D, Twenty-Fifth Infantry.[53]

Even though U.S. Army personnel worked hard to keep a
bridge across the Pecos, they could not subdue the river. On August
15, 1880, a lieutenant wired Fort Concho that the Pecos at Camp
Melvin was "up and impassable. It is about one half mile wide and
still rising. Bridge has broken loose from the west bank and swung
over to east bank. It is probable that three of the boats can be fixed.
One is sunk. Part of the flooring has been lost, some new will be
needed."[54]

On September 9, stage agents relayed to Major R. F.
O'Beirne of Fort Stockton that the bridge was now passable, despite
"a constant change tak[ing] place in the river owing to frequent
rains." Nevertheless, a returning detachment reported to O'Beirne
four days later that the river remained "very high and bridge in need
of repairs. . . . New sleepers [support beams] and one new boat are
badly needed. Also seventy-five feet of chain, half-inch link. Rope is
now being used in place of chain."[55]

By September 28, the Pecos had subsided, and wagon trains
had resumed crossing the bridge.[56]

With the Apache threat diminishing, Fort Stockton's commander reduced the picket at Camp Melvin to a single noncommissioned officer and two privates by January 1880. By March, even
these were gone,[57] and by the close of 1881, so, too, was Pontoon
Bridge's singular importance.[58] The Texas & Pacific Railroad had
bridged not just the Pecos, but the entirety of Texas from east to west,
opening up a new era.

With the stage company suddenly stripped of its lifeblood
mail contract, the very future of Pontoon Bridge came under threat.
For several years, already, the U.S. Army and the stage company had
squabbled over control of the structure. On October 15, 1875, for
example, Captain S. T. Norvell of Fort Stockton had petitioned
Department of Texas headquarters to relay instructions on "what
action I can take in case of a refusal on the part of the stage company to allow [military] mail parties to use the bridge."[59] Therefore,

when a January 16, 1882, rumor held that the stage company had sold the bridge to "Mr. Torres" (likely Cesario Torres) and that he intended to dismantle it, Colonel Benjamin Grierson of Fort Concho immediately telegraphed the commander at Stockton.

"The boats have been built and the bridge kept in repair by the government, and in my opinion no one has any right to take it away so long as the government requires it[s] use . . . ," said Grierson. "I recommend that steps be taken to prevent the removal of this bridge."[60]

Whatever the truth of the rumor, the bridge lingered as a noted landmark, even as the rock walls of Camp Melvin crumbled. As early as 1873, when George Owens accompanied Colonel Ranald Mackenzie up the Pecos, two brothers named Roberts grazed cattle near Pontoon Crossing and made their home in a dugout.[61] And when a bad winter in northern territories spawned the Big Drift of cattle to the lower Pecos in 1885, cattlemen chose Pontoon as the starting point for a massive roundup that began May 20.[62]

The unavoidable overgrazing and an ensuing drought crippled ranching interests on the Pecos, but rains eventually rejuvenated the range. The grasses lured not only more cattlemen, but also sheepmen such as A. D. Locklin, who grazed his flocks in the lowlands adjacent to Pontoon in the 1890s.

"He ran sheep under herd . . . on the free range," recalled his daughter-in-law Nora Locklin in 1992. "He didn't have a certain place. He had a Mexican [herder]. And they would run as much as twenty thousand sheep at one time."[63]

On into the 1900s, emigrants and wagoners continued to take advantage of this easiest of all frontier crossings of the Pecos.

"It was pretty popular back when I was a kid," recalled Cliff Newland, who was born in 1886. "I know some of the [James] Curries, [for whom Newland worked], when they had to go back and forth in the buckboard to see about their sheep, they'd go by Pontoon Crossing on account of the bridge."[64]

In 1904, young Opal Nix and her family, in two wagons and a hack, headed west to her father Tom Hickox's forty-section ranch across the Pecos.

"We had loaded wagons . . . and some chickens tied under the hack . . . ," Mrs. Nix recalled in 1968. "We rode horseback part of the time, drove this little herd of horses."

As they neared the Pecos, they met up with cowhand

George Lee, who directed them past the Holmsley Ranch and down JM Draw to the river.

"[We] crossed at Pontoon Crossing . . . ," she remembered. "I thought rivers had trees on them, and that [Pecos] just looked like a little ol' branch—but we had such a hard time getting across. We were told that there's lots of quicksand. . . .

"We were so tired when we finally made it across. . . . It was in June, and it was hot, and we kids just fell off of that wagon—it was loaded just real high, with sideboards on it—and fell into the mesquite flats and ate those mesquite beans just like cattle. Oh, they tasted so good."[65]

Although Pontoon Bridge doubtlessly deteriorated steadily after the abandonment of Fort Stockton in 1886, folklore incredibly holds that early automobiles rumbled across in the early twentieth century.

"They started the town of Buena Vista back in the late 1890s or early 1900s," noted historian Ed Bartholomew. "Promoters—a man named Draper was the main salesman—got up a huge emigrant party from the Middle West, came . . . to San Angelo . . . and rented every car in town. It must've been 1906 or 1907, along in there. And they made this one hundred fifty-mile trip to the Pecos. They crossed at Pontoon, according to the reminiscences, in automobiles. They came to the new town of Buena Vista . . . and [the promoters] took them out to sell them irrigated farms."[66]

Floods and continued deterioration soon left the bridge in shambles. Surveyor Bill Drake reported on November 19, 1911, that he had inspected the site and found little evidence of the structure. "On the bank of the river, south of the house [Camp Melvin] some thirty varas [83 feet], I found a large rock with tool marks on it and a circle of iron rust around it. . . . Presumably it was one of the bridge anchors. Slope from house to bank is steep. Northwest of anchor we found part of what seemed to have been the retaining wall, and in the river we found a partly submerged old pontoon. . . . On the left bank of the Pecos [I] found the walls of the old stage stand, roof gone."[67]

In 1920, surveyor J. D. Freeman reported finding only remnants of the bridge pilings, with heavy chain attached.[68] Repeated floods during the next quarter-century further decimated the structure.

"After World War II, I walked that side of the river . . . and where Pontoon was, I crawled down kind of a bluff," recalled Bartholomew. "In the bank was one of these iron hitching rings for the east end of that floating bridge. They put boats in the water, and then bolted a bridge across it, and so it had to be anchored."[69]

In 1955, when Tom Vandevanter first rode horseback along the Pecos at Camp Melvin, he found only a series of posts where the bridge had stretched back up onto the east bank. Then came a major flood a decade and a half later, cutting out the bank, changing the river's course.

"I saw one windmill that you could just barely see the top, up on that Five Mile Draw just before you get to the river," recalled Vandevanter, who added that the flood waters "washed a lot" around the stage stand.[70]

Today, only a pair of rotting posts marks Pontoon Crossing's eastern bank.[71] And although Camp Melvin, as well, is slowly succumbing to time, legends of nearby treasure remain strong.

Ford Armstrong claimed in 1959 that loot from the robbery of an army paymaster lay buried at or near the crossing and that an acquaintance had dug up $62,000 at the site. Authorities in Juarez, Mexico, he added, had arrested the man when he had tried to dispose of $18,000 in gold. Joe E. Blumentritt, holding to another version of the tale, asserted in 1961 that the treasure was from the long-ago robbery of a Southern Pacific train.[72]

As Vandevanter heard the story, the outlaw loot in the Camp Melvin vicinity is that of Black Jack Ketchum and his gang,[73] whom newspapers of the day credited with the May 14, 1897, robbery of a Southern Pacific train at Lozier Canyon. The outlaws eluded a posse, and authorities never recovered the missing $6,000 or more.[74]

Black Jack Ketchum. (J. Evetts Haley Collection, N. S. Haley Memorial Library, Midland, Texas)

"To the east of [Camp Melvin], as you're going in the mountains, I heard people have even found packsaddles," related Vandevanter, whose ranch extends into those rugged hills. "Now, myself, I haven't found any packsaddles, but I do know of some caves back there, and they are supposedly where the Ketchums hung out."

The caves or overhangs, said Vandevanter, are located near the old stage road. "The very best one—that I always assumed that they had found something in—is caved in," he noted. "But there's another one that has Indian writings and you can still distinguish them. But the markings and writings [have] diminished pretty greatly the last few years."[75]

To credulous treasure hunters, such writings may be more than Indian rock art—they may represent clues to hidden bonanzas such as that which reportedly inspired a deathbed map by an elderly Mexican many decades ago.

Pursued by Texas Rangers down the old stage road between the Middle Concho and Camp Melvin about 1900, the man supposedly took refuge at dusk in a shallow cave on the great ridge overlooking Pontoon Crossing from the east. He awoke the next morning to find a stack of silver ingots where the cave twisted back into the rock. He seized two ingots and fled on horseback, committing to memory every landmark as he rode—the nearby burned wagon irons, Pontoon Crossing in the distance, and the Pecos valley spreading out in a great Y.

Captured that morning with the ingots still in his possession, the man kept his silence, as he did through long years of imprisonment. Finally realizing he was dying, he entrusted his secret to a kindly jailer and sketched a map.[76] It shows the Pecos River's serpentine journey down from Horsehead Crossing to Pontoon, and, immediately east of the old bridge, wagon irons just below a cave marked by an X. According to the sketch, the treasure cave lies in a bluff just south of the old Fort Stockton-to-Santa Rita road.[77] The fact that Santa Rita is included as a landmark indicates that the map was drawn sometime after the Santa Rita #1 discovery oil well blew in on May 28, 1923, in Reagan County.[78]

Musty and garbled, the tales nevertheless pay tribute to the role of Camp Melvin and Pontoon Bridge in opening the frontier. Although crumbling—in the case of Camp Melvin—and already gone—in the case of Pontoon Bridge—they have risen out of the dust of history to gain immortality in the folklore of the West. ★

Into a sun setting over a land cursed by thirst, men and mules struggled, weak and exhausted.

It was Monday, March 5, 1849. For Captain William H. C. Whiting and his command, it was a moment of desperation. Three weeks before, they had forged west from San Antonio to blaze a road toward El Paso, but now the want of water ruled them.

On this day alone, their mules had carried them thirty-five miles, and every stride took them farther from the last sure water, already one hundred miles and three days behind at the head of the San Saba River. With their animals faltering and thirst raging, they had no choice but to push on into the night for the Pecos that they hoped lay ahead.

"How weary were the miles of that last march!" Whiting wrote in his journal. "Silent, unmurmuring, each man rode on, his weary mule unable to make more than a mile and a half an hour."

On into midnight the party staggered, across tableland falling away, down an old trail, through a ravine. Finally, forty-two brutal miles from their last camp, the hard dark yielded the sound of rippling water—Live Oak Creek, a Pecos tributary.

Surviving, they lay up a day and a half and pushed on five miles down a recent Indian trail to the Pecos, which squirmed through a deep valley a mile wide. Scouting just downstream near present Sheffield, they reached a side canyon that opened up across the river; it spilled out of five-hundred-foot mountains and paved the banks and river bed with gravel, rendering the Pecos firm and shallow—a ford![1]

For the next half-century, this passage across the deadly river was the crucial link to the West not only for the Lower Road—Whiting's general route—but also for an eventual coast-to-coast trail that opened up the frontier to thousands of travelers. Yet, strangely, the ford never gained an enduring name, although terms for it were many—Lancaster Crossing,[2] Pecos Crossing,[3] Solomon's Ford,[4] Indian Ford,[5] Crossing of the Pecos,[6] Crossing Rio Pecos,[7] Ferry of the Pecos,[8] Ford Canyon Crossing.[9]

No one knows the names by which war-mongering Indians knew Lancaster Crossing, though their horses splashed across it regularly long before Whiting's expedition. Indeed, his junior officer, Brevet Second Lieutenant William F. Smith, noted that the ford "appears to be frequently used by the Indians, in their incursions into Mexico,"[10] while Whiting noted that the approaching trail bore "the bones of horses and cattle, scraps of cloth, small articles dropped here and there, [that] told of some hapless captive and the late march of a band of the plunderers of Mexico."[11]

As soon as the army pinpointed Lancaster Crossing as a key objective on the lower route west, it proved little more forgiving to travelers than to captives. Although Whiting found it only waist deep, the surging current easily upended men afoot and forced even mules to swim. Turning to three small islands just upstream, Whiting erected a crude footbridge of live oak logs and crossed his command.[12]

Beyond the Pecos, the terrain ruled out a direct push west, forcing an initial thirty-eight-mile trek upstream, a journey that Whiting likened to a virtual march through hell. "Few landscapes," he reported, "can be conceived more bleak and utterly desolate, in its monotonous and somber features, its destitution of trees and foliage, than the Pecos country affords. Even game seem to shun it."[13]

Captain S. G. French, reaching Lancaster Crossing later that year, shared Whiting's impressions. "Few places," he wrote, "can be found more solitary, or that present a more dreary appearance, than all this region of the Pecos." He noted that neither a tree nor bush marked the river, and that a person could "stand on its banks and not know that the stream is near." Furthermore, the banks were so uniformly steep that "in a course of two hundred and forty miles, there are but few places where an animal can approach them for water in safety."[14]

By the end of 1849, the Lower Road, with its official military travel, had become a viable passage west, regularly carrying wagoners 673 miles between San Antonio and El Paso.[15] As refined, the route included vital water sources at Howard's Wells (or Springs) thirty-nine miles southeast of Lancaster Crossing and at Pecos Springs five miles upstream.[16] Unlike the Upper Road, which was twenty-seven miles shorter,[17] the southern route avoided Horsehead Crossing and the Comanche war trail. Nevertheless, Indian attack grew so common on the Lower Road that within eight years an army lieutenant would lament, "Scarcely a mile of it but has its story of Indian murder and plunder; in fact, from El Paso to San Antonio is but one long battle ground."[18]

Hostiles plundered even large parties, as six hundred California-bound emigrants learned in 1850.

"Our caravan made a train some three miles long, as we had ninety-five wagons with two to three yoke of oxen to each wagon," remembered J. Frank Bowles years later. "We had about five hundred head of work oxen, besides the horses. . . . The Indians would often steal into the herd [at night] and stampede them."

Reaching Lancaster Crossing, the wagoners halted and planned an assault on its waters.

"We rested several days," wrote Bowles, "and built large rafts to carry the wagons over. The river being narrow, we had no trouble in crossing the stock."[19]

By the fall of 1851, Henry Skillman's wagoners dared Lancaster Crossing once a month in carrying both citizen and military mail between San Antonio and Santa Fe. Without relay stations to provide fresh teams, Skillman's employees herded relief teams along and rested the animals at night. Passenger fare from El Paso to San Antonio was $100.[20]

To guard the route to the ford and beyond, the U.S. Army in 1852 established Fort Clark[21] 174 miles southeast.[22] In 1853, army inspector Colonel Joseph K. F. Mansfield found the 544 miles between Fort Clark and San Elizario (near El Paso) "without a settlement of *any description*." Yet, he noted, the trade "that is carried on over this route is great: it is one of the overland routes to California and to Chihuahua, and across this route the Indians travel at different points to commit their depredations on the Mexicans."

Mansfield recommended Live Oak Creek near Lancaster Crossing for one of three posts "as places of protection and resort to travellers in distress." He cited the location's "abundance of grazing, wood, and *good* water" and noted that relays of mules at such a post could facilitate twice-a-month mail runs.[23]

While the army mulled over his proposal, thousands of cattle retraced the Lower Road west to Lancaster Crossing en route to California and ready markets at mining camps. James Campbell of San Antonio, who made a successful four-month drive from Eagle Pass to a ranch near San Diego in 1853, noted in a memorandum the scarcity of watering places along the canal-like Pecos.[24]

"After crossing the Pacus [sic] six or seven miles you will find a spring [Pecos Spring] to the right in some chaparral. Ten miles from the crossing of the Pacus you will find a watering place [on the river] at the mouth of a hollow, gravelly beach. From that point five or six miles, another watering place one-half mile before you get to the bluff of a mountain.

"From there, look out for best places to water."[25]

Campbell again drove a herd over the Texas-California Cattle Trail in 1854,[26] a year that marked the height of activity along the route. On May 26, the *Galveston Journal* reported that "large droves of beef cattle continue to be driven from Western Texas for California. A drove of seven hundred head passed through Victoria a few days since."[27] Two months later, the *Colorado Tribune* of Texas observed that "the speculation of driving beef cattle from our State to California still continues, and doubtless a regular trade will be made of it for some years to come."[28]

On April 23 or 24 of that year, Michael Erskine set out from South Texas with 1,054 beeves. By the time the drovers neared Live Oak Creek and "the Station"—a temporary army encampment and precursor to Mansfield's proposed post—violent storms and stampedes had cut the herd to 932 head. Crossing the beeves at Lancaster Crossing on June 14 with "no misfortune of any kind," recorded Erskine in his diary, he pushed on for California. Six months and a few days after departing, he reached Warner's Ranch near San Diego with 814 animals.[29]

Twelve days behind the Erskine herd, a drove owned by John James also forded Lancaster Crossing, which twenty-two-year-old drover James G. Bell described in his diary. "This stream," he wrote, "is turbulent and rapid [and] the color is a rich pink. . . . The banks are high and dangerous for cattle; depth from five to ten feet." Indeed, the following morning the drovers suffered beef losses to the river while watering the herd a few miles upstream. Soon afterward,

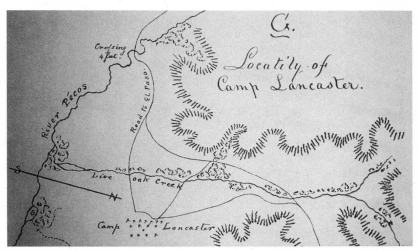

Colonel J. K. Mansfield's 1856 map of Fort Lancaster and Lancaster Crossing.
(courtesy, Fort Lancaster State Historical Park)

in readying to strike out west from the Pecos and its pitfalls, Bell observed that "[I] am sure no one of the party will regret it in the least."[30]

Lancaster Crossing and the Pecos gained an eastern sentinel August 20, 1855, when Captain S. D. Carpenter and companies H and K of the First Infantry—in response to orders issued a month earlier—occupied a site on Live Oak Creek four to five miles away. [31] Designated "Camp Lancaster," the lonely outpost lay midway between San Antonio and El Paso, and 158 miles east of Fort Davis, [32] a Lower Road post set up in 1854.[33]

From the start, Camp Lancaster's forces met resistance from Indians along the Pecos. In late fall 1855, infantrymen repelled an attack by hostiles near the post and gained the praise of superiors at Department of Texas headquarters.[34]

The following June, Colonel Mansfield personally inspected the camp—by then garrisoned with three officers and 150 enlisted men—and hailed it as "indispensable to travellers and in a locality often visited by the wild Indians traversing the country. . . . At this place travellers can rest and recruit their animals and repair their wagons with safety. It undoubtedly has and will save many valuable lives."[35]

That very season, noted Mansfield, Apaches had attacked a

New Mexico-bound wagon train approximately eighty-nine miles southeast of Lancaster, killing one man and severely wounding another. Army detachments had escorted the beleaguered emigrants to Lancaster Crossing and on to Fort Davis.

"But for my timely arrival, and the aid of this post [Lancaster]," wrote Mansfield, "these men would have been murdered and their cows and calves . . . captured by the Indians."

Labeling Apaches the "highway men" of the region, Mansfield noted that they "keep out of sight and commit depredations and murders at times when least expected. They are on the Pecos, in the mountains, on Devils river, &c [etc.], always concealed and difficult to find." He recommended that the army mount one Lancaster company on mules "so as to be able to trail Indians after they [have] . . . committed depredations" and urged superiors to arm each infantryman with the new rifled musket. "Indians when running," he pointed out, "must be reached at a long range, up the mountains &c, or not at all."

Noting Camp Lancaster's strategic location—"about one-half way between forts Davis and Clark"—Mansfield observed that, with the number of far-ranging hostiles beyond estimate, "it is quite probable that this and other posts will have to be maintained for a great many years."[36]

Perhaps spurred by Mansfield's statement, the army directed on August 21, 1856, that "the post known as Camp Lancaster . . . will be considered on the same footing with regard to permanency as the other frontier posts in the Department, and will in the future be called Fort Lancaster."[37]

Despite the new designation, emigrants still faced Indian threat along the nearby Pecos. Immediately upon fording Lancaster Crossing with fifteen men and one woman bound for the Gadsden Purchase in the fall of 1856, "Colonel" Palatine Robinson turned his horse off-trail after game and fell behind. Loping the animal in order to rejoin his party, he soon caught sight of the two hindmost riders across a dry creek. As his mount carefully picked its way down into the ravine, it suddenly shied at the whistling of arrows. Whirling down-creek to the shielding folds of the banks, Robinson found his attackers, yet the rearing of his horse prevented him from shooting back.

Desperate and trapped, he regained control of the animal and, drawing his repeating pistols, fired as he spurred his horse straight for his foes. He felled several outright, and when the others took flight, he pursued them down the ravine until he had emptied his guns.[38]

In 1857, traveler John C. Reid avoided bloodshed at the crossing, though he learned the Pecos held its own dangers. "We found much difficulty in fording . . . ," he recorded. "I would suggest as the most approved way of crossing this ford from this way [the east], to enter the stream opposite to the head of the island, and drive directly thereto, thence diagonally with the stream to the going out place."

Proceeding upstream, Reid and his party discovered another hazard of the Pecos—its alkaline waters. "We heard much of it killing work animals," he wrote, "and losing two of our mules when on it, came to the conclusion that their drinking it terminated their existence."[39]

That summer, Lancaster Crossing witnessed the strangest of all caravans—camels bearing the brand of the U.S. Army. The first of these westbound "ships of the desert" reached Live Oak Creek on July 9 and crossed the next day at the ford, which Lieutenant Edward Fitzgerald Beale described as a "turbid, swift running stream, of about three feet in depth and twenty-five in width, the water of which is . . . unpleasant to both sight and taste."[40] May Humphreys Stacey, a nineteen-year-old civilian accompanying the party, reported that the eight-mile-per-hour current carried muddy water "much thicker than the Mississippi, and so brackish that the mules will hardly drink it."[41]

For two days, as men, camels, and mules worked their way upstream between castellated hills, the proximity of Pecos water teased the animals while the sharp banks frustrated their handlers. Finally, Beale breathed a sigh of relief.

"We leave the Pecos this evening, and are all glad of it," he wrote on July 12. "A more stupid and uninteresting river cannot be imagined—rapid, muddy, brackish, timberless, and hard to get at."[42]

Its turbid nature proved especially worrisome to an army corporal on march with Zenas R. Bliss in the spring of 1858. Fording Lancaster Crossing en route east from Fort Davis, Bliss and his command found the river only about two feet deep. "But," wrote Bliss, "owing to the muddy character of the water, we could not see the bottom, and one of the men, Corporal Thorpe, was frightened nearly to death while wading across; he had to be supported by the other men, who laughed at him for his fears." A year later, Thorpe committed suicide rather than ford the Devil's River east of Lancaster.[43]

Despite the perils of the Pecos, Lancaster Crossing proved vital to the transcontinental mail company of James E. Birch, whose first wagon rolled out of San Antonio on July 9, 1857, and forded at the site en route 1,475 miles to San Diego, California. The second mail, and the first by four-horse coach, followed on August 1 in the charge of Henry Skillman, who had yielded his original mail line to George H. Giddings of San Antonio in 1854. Skillman's party, including line superintendent J. C. Woods, reached the Fort Lancaster vicinity August 7 and crossed the ford the next day. Camping nightly, the group still averaged forty miles a day and reached the West Coast on September 8.

In his report to the postmaster general, Woods noted the line's importance to emigrants.

"Wood, water, and grass, are the emigrant's necessities in crossing our continent . . . ," he wrote. "An emigrant passing over our route will meet or be overtaken by a mail party four times every month, while from our mail conductors he can always obtain the reliable information as to road, wood, water, grass, camping places . . . and transmit messages [or] letters."

Still, mail parties, like emigrant parties, faced the lurking threat of hostiles between San Antonio and El Paso. In reporting that Indians "occasionally" made themselves known, Woods noted that they "have never but once made an attack upon the [wagon] train."[44]

On that occasion, in July 1857, Indians ambushed the W. A. A. "Bigfoot" Wallace party as it pushed relay teams over the route to Fort Lancaster in advance of Skillman's first stage. When the mules bolted to the gunfire, Wallace and a man named Clifford jumped from the coach to help the drovers hold the animals. As Clifford ran, he suffered a severe wound and fell back to die in hand-to-hand combat. Wallace, meanwhile, managed to turn the mules from the road, only to find the war party at his flank. Giving up the herd, Wallace narrowly escaped on a saddle mule. Although a Fort Clark cavalry patrol later recovered many of the animals, they no longer were fit for stage purposes.[45]

Upon Birch's untimely death in a steamship disaster later in 1857, Giddings and R. E. Doyle took over the semi-monthly service [46] and set passenger fare from New Orleans to San Francisco at $200. To allay fears of Indian attack, they advertised that "an armed escort travels through the Indian country with each mail train, for the protection of the mails and passengers."[47]

Fort Lancaster, the only outpost for hundreds of miles, stood out as indispensable to the San Antonio-San Diego Mail. On June 4, 1858, the army directed the post commander to allow the company to build nearby sheds for their animals. On October 30 of that year, military authorities ordered Forts Lancaster and Davis to protect the mail line, and, two months later, directed that the two posts jointly establish a picket for that purpose at Escondido Springs, sixty-five miles by stage road northwest of Lancaster Crossing.[48] Then, in 1859, Fort Lancaster gave birth to the Pecos River's western guardian—Camp (or Fort) Stockton—when Company H set up stakes nineteen miles northwest of Escondido at Comanche Springs.[49]

Sometime during this period, the U.S. Army or the San Antonio-San Diego Mail—or both—may have spanned Lancaster Crossing with a bridge, for military correspondence of November 1867 makes reference to "the bridge formerly thrown over it of iron." Nevertheless, the crossing proved unyielding, for the same enigmatic letter notes ambiguously that the structure "was destroyed some years ago."[50]

Despite military posts on both sides of the Pecos, the Indian menace grew worse. On November 21, 1860, Colonel Mansfield reported that Fort Lancaster occupied "a highly important position in the midst of Indian depredations. About six weeks [ago] . . . two men were murdered by them about ten miles off on the Pecos, and a few days [ago] . . . four Indians ran off seven mules of the stage company, which has a station here."[51] Only a month or so after his inspection, a Lancaster contingent in the charge of a Sergeant Spangler skirmished Indians on the Pecos.[52]

A sketch of Fort Lancaster made by a government draftsman about 1860.
(courtesy, Fort Lancaster State Historical Park)

More than a skirmish, however, brewed throughout the nation. On February 24, 1861, the day after Texas voted overwhelmingly to secede from the Union and align with the Confederacy, the U.S. Army ordered the evacuation of Fort Lancaster and other Lower Road posts in Texas.[53] While the garrisons at the Trans-Pecos forts of Bliss, Quitman, Davis, and Stockton proceeded with the evacuation and long march toward Lancaster Crossing and the Texas coast, Captain Robert Granger and his command fled Fort Lancaster under a cloud of violence. On the very day of departure, March 19, a Private Cunningham fell to a bullet fired by David Ramsey, an employee of the San Antonio-San Diego Mail.[54]

It would not be the last violence within earshot of Lancaster Crossing during the next four years of civil war. Not only did hostiles again rage unchecked along the Pecos, but also, before war's end, a nighttime clash between Union and Rebel forces would bloody a hill near Fort Lancaster.

To protect the Confederacy's stake in the Lower Road, W. P. Lane's Rangers—officially mustered as Company F, Second Texas Mounted Rifles at Marshall in May 1861—occupied Fort Lancaster on November 6. Twenty-two days later Confederate Brigadier General H. H. Sibley, bound for New Mexico with hopes of conquering the West, inspected Fort Lancaster's garrison on the parade ground at seven in the morning. Armed and mounted, Lane's Rangers responded a little too enthusiastically when Sibley took charge to see how well they had been drilled.

"Sergeant Harwell was on the right, marching by two's," Lane Ranger W. W. Heartsill reported in his journal. "The command was given by the general, 'file left,' which was of course unheard, and on they went at a brisk trot, ascended the mountain, and as they disappeared the general turned around muttering 'gone to h—l.'"

The company did not return until evening, by which time Sibley already had forded Lancaster Crossing and "gone on his way rejoicing to New Mexico,"[55] where his hopes of claiming the West for the Confederacy would die in the snows of Glorieta Pass in March 1862.

Despite the Civil War, stages continued to struggle across Lancaster Crossing in the winter of 1861-1862 in making the run between San Antonio and Santa Fe. On January 14, 1862, Lancaster's troops learned from eastbound stage personnel that smallpox had struck Fort Davis and that Indians had burned Pecos

Mail Station, a stage stand upstream of the ford. Eleven days later, the San Antonio stage rumbled down the six-hundred-foot mountain to the east and delivered copies of the *Texas Republican*, which included Heartsill's December 29, 1861, letter to the editor. In lamenting the deaths of fellow soldiers, including one who lay buried at Fort Lancaster, Heartsill wrote:

"Tis true they fell not in the fierce battle strife, but they fell nobly at their post, where their country called them; and every honest heart will give a sympathetic sigh, while we mourn over the loss of our fellow soldiers and commit them to the silent tomb, far away from home and kind kindred. A grave at every post, with one exception, to remind us that life is but a span."[56]

Although a company of the Second Regiment from Fort Stockton relieved Lane's Rangers on April 11, 1862,[57] it was a temporary assignment, because the embattled Confederacy decided against a constant presence at Fort Lancaster and along the Lower Road west. In mid-winter 1864, the situation led U.S. Army General H. W. Halleck to order troops from New Mexico Territory to march down the Rio Grande into Texas. Reaching the Lower Road, they were to cooperate with Union forces approaching from the Texas coast in blocking the road and preventing "any trade or communication between rebels in Texas and their friends in Mexican territory." A third set of Union troops, consisting of four companies of the First California Cavalry, already had been dispatched eastward from California, and three additional companies soon would join them.[58]

In mid-March, Confederate headquarters in Texas learned that a 500-man Union force from California had encamped on the Pecos River near Fort Lancaster. From that base, the Yankees reportedly were raiding the area and attracting Union sympathizers and Confederate deserters. Texas Governor Pendleton Murrah immediately ordered the Frontier Rangers to intercept the force. With approximately 550 Rangers, Major J. M. Hunter headed west on April 8.

Reaching a stream within twenty miles of Fort Lancaster on April 17, Hunter held his command in camp while he and three men scouted ahead during the night. They found the post deserted, but a well-beaten trail led them southward to the Californians' tents on a wooded bluff with two near-precipitous sides. Riding until the following noon to rejoin his command, Hunter rested the Rangers the remainder of the day and marched out after sundown. Positioning forces on opposing slopes of the Californians' stronghold, they attacked the sleeping army by moonlight and bloodied the night, killing thirty-five soldiers and severely wounding twenty more. Although fourteen Rangers dropped to gunfire, with eight eventually dying of their wounds, the Texas victory was so decisive that the Californians fled into Mexico and never again threatened the Lower Road.[59]

Even though Confederate General Robert E. Lee's surrender on April 9, 1865, marked the end of war and insured the unity of the nation, more than two years passed before the U.S. Army reestablished on the Pecos. In the spring and summer of 1867, preparatory to reactivation of Lower Road posts, Captain Edward S. Meyer surveyed from San Antonio to El Paso. Finding Fort Lancaster in ruins, he proceeded to "Crossing Rio Pecos" (or Lancaster Crossing) and noted its advantages and perils.

"Good camping ground on either bank of the Rio, with sufficient wood for fuel," he noted. "Fair grazing, an abundance of good though muddy water in the Rio. The crossing is ordinarily about three feet deep, but is often so high, and rapid, as to be impassable for a train for several days."[60]

Upon reoccupying Fort Stockton eighty-four miles northwest on July 7, 1867,[61] the U.S. Army soon met with freight losses and delays at the ford. Still, by mid-November, mail wagons made the difficult crossing under escort from a picket at Fort Lancaster, which the army had relegated to the status of temporary subpost despite Stockton commander Edward Hatch's argument that it was "as important as any point on the line, more so than the post at Davis." The situation prompted army plans for a bridge.

"This bridge is greatly needed," wrote Hatch on November 18 in acknowledging orders for its construction. "The crossing, a bad one, is often impracticable from high water. Apart from the delay which is thus occasioned, already government stores enough have been destroyed this season by water to build it."[62]

On December 9, Hatch dispatched thirty-five carpenters to the nearest timber—the mountainous pine forests north of Fort Davis—and charged them with building the bridge for later removal to the Pecos. By letter, he asked Fort Davis's commander, James F. Wade, to ready the required lumber.

"It will require about 3,000 feet board measure," wrote Hatch. "The plank should be twelve (12) feet long, two and one-half

(2 1/2) inches thick. This bridge is of great importance to all posts west of it, and any assistance you can give is important to Fort Davis as well as Stockton."[63]

Hatch reiterated the structure's significance in correspondence to District of Texas headquarters December 14. "The bridge," he said, "is important and worth to the government ten times its cost nearly."[64]

While the bridge steadily took shape at the hands of carpenters and Stockton quartermaster Jacob Humfreville,[65] one of the Pecos's most violent army-Indian confrontations occurred at Fort Lancaster, where black "buffalo" soldiers and white officers of Company K, Ninth Cavalry, had encamped. But for the whimsical choice of a spooked horse herd to flee south for the river, the confrontation could have been a massacre to rival that of General George Armstrong Custer and his command at Little Big Horn.

It was about 4:00 p.m. on the day after Christmas, 1867. As the horse herd—in the charge of mounted guards—passed through camp en route from pasture to water, two hundred Indians, Mexicans, and white renegades swooped down from the north by horseback and stampeded the animals. The guards opened fire, but superior numbers quickly dragged them from their mounts. Sixty attackers swept on through the startled soldiers, who soon gathered themselves and herded the majority of the horses toward the corral, only to find bars blocking it and another enemy wave charging from the west.

With the battle spreading, the soldiers took positions to the north, west, and south, while company commander William Frohock and a contingent fought their way across to the horse herd. However,

Brevet Lieutenant Colonel William Frohock.
(courtesy, Fort Lancaster State Historical Park)

reported Frohock, "such . . . was the panic among the [horses] and so close upon us were the savages, that it was found impossible to control them long enough to open the corral."

Falling back to the ruins of the sutler's store, the main body of soldiers finally repulsed the attack from the north, but found the west force—buoyed by the sixty riders who had swept through camp—fast closing around the horses.

"I proceeded with every available man against them," wrote Frohock, "but before anything definite could be accomplished, the frightened horses rushed southward through our line and through that of another force numbering from three to four hundred which was advancing upon us from that direction."

With attack only moments away on a third front, the stampede proved the difference between life and death for Company K.

"Had this stampede not occurred," wrote Frohock, "it is doubtful if the defense against such overwhelming odds could have been successful."

With the horses—the objective of the attack—now behind its lines, the southern body of Indians-renegades withdrew and formed a mile-wide battle front between the soldiers and animals. Refusing to accept the loss of the herd, Frohock left only a few men in camp and deployed the remainder as skirmishers. He wrote:

"I advanced upon their lines which, receiving our fire, broke and reformed to the rear, several times; always, however, keeping the horses behind them and themselves beyond the reach of our shots."

Suddenly hearing renewed hostilities at camp, Frohock sent a sergeant and ten men on in pursuit while he quickly fell back with the balance of his command to face a second attack from the north. For long, desperate minutes, the soldiers fought fiercely in and around the ruins before finally repelling the band.

By now, large bodies of additional warriors and renegades—two-thirds of them unmounted—had appeared on the surrounding hills and in a nearby canyon. Learning only then that his command had faced an incredible army of 900 to 1,500 warriors, Frohock realized just how close he and his men had come to massacre.

"Every disposition indicated a simultaneous attack from all sides to have been intended, but after the stampede of the horses their object seemed accomplished and the Indians upon the hillsides and in the valleys south and west of camp made no further demonstrations, although several hundreds appeared in full view."

Nightfall brought the return of the men who had been sent in pursuit of the horses; they had kept up the chase for four miles before running out of ammunition and yielding to the dark. The night also gave Frohock a chance to count his losses: three men missing and presumed dead, including a teamster who, in the company of four men, had been acquiring wood and water near a live oak grove when the battle had erupted. "The teamster William Sharps," he reported, "saw the Indians and gave warning in time for the others to secrete themselves, defense being impracticable, as the Indians were between them and camp. But before he could get away from his team, he was lassoed." Frohock further determined that the war party had escaped with thirty-two horses and six mules, while five more horses lay dead or wounded among the ruins.

Although Frohock initially assessed Indian-renegade losses at two men killed and several wounded, a few days later Fort Stockton commander Hatch amended the fatality figure to an "estimated twenty." Exact enemy losses were impossible to determine, said Hatch, "as night enabled them to recover their killed and wounded."

The most striking thing about the military-like attack had been the participation of white men—apparently ex-Confederates carrying on the fight that had ended for most soldiers thirty-two months before. "The leader who charged with the first party appeared to be a white man . . . ," noted Frohock. "The men [at the live oak grove] who escaped report that there were white men among them who spoke English draped in Confederate uniforms." Hatch, in describing the number of Caucasians as "many," likewise stressed that "conspicuous among the white men was the rebel uniform." Among the items soon recovered from the field of battle was one "private's infantry coat," presumably Confederate. Conversely, the bodies of the three slain U.S. Army soldiers would not be located for three months.

On the night of December 28, two days after the battle, a war party again stormed Fort Lancaster—this time with far less force—but failed to capture the remaining stock. Finally, the band fled down the Pecos. "The Indians attacking Lancaster have moved south, will probably go into Mexico and then attack the settlements east of Fort Duncan," Hatch reported on January 3. "They had with them a large number of American horses and mules, evidently taken from settlements or posts west of us."[66]

Despite the Indian situation on the Lower Road, which Hatch assessed as "very troublesome," by February 20, 1868, carpenters in the Davis Mountains had completed the long-awaited bridge and the army prepared to carry it by wagon to the Pecos.[67] In March, the transport wagons, under the guard of a detachment of Company K, Ninth Cavalry, screeched to a halt on the banks of the river.[68] The site chosen was not Lancaster Crossing, but instead a straightaway a mile or two upstream[69] where the valley's defining bluffs withdrew a little.

By March 28, the bridge was in place,[70] a structure less than sixty-five feet in length,[71] yet one spanning a river that already had coursed hundreds of miles from the snow-capped Sangre de Cristo range in New Mexico. From the start, Fort Stockton realized that a picket was essential to guard military and citizen interests. In late March or early April, a sergeant and twelve men of Company D, Ninth Cavalry, armed with one hundred rounds each, relieved the detachment of Company K at the bridge. The thirteen soldiers of Company D, in turn, would be relieved in thirty days.[72]

As the seasons passed, however, the tours of duty grew increasingly long, despite the isolation of the bridge and the primitive living conditions in which guards quartered in three huts lining the east bank just upstream.[73] In his late September 1868 inspection of the sanitary condition of the picket, by then reduced to twelve men, Fort Stockton post surgeon R. Lauszky was aghast. He reported:

> I found the men stationed there in a ragged half-naked condition! Some of them had not a single shirt and consequently none on their backs; others were barefooted! Imagine a United States soldier barefooted, without a shirt on his back, covering his nakedness with a remnant of an old piece of rag, which might have been once . . . an infantry blouse! And you have a rudely drawn picture of the cavalry soldiers stationed at the Pecos Bridge!

In recommending that the army relieve the detachments every two to three months, Lauszky observed: "Not being under the supervision of commissioned officers, they become entirely demoralized! Having nothing to do, they become insolent, vulgar, profane, neglectful, filthy, and consequently inefficient, and I doubt not sick from mere inactivity and exposure. . . . I cannot but think that they sell their clothing to the trains, passing by, otherwise I could not account for their wretched condition."[74]

Although the Lancaster bridge gave Lower Road travelers easy passage across the Pecos, it did nothing to ease the burden of fording on the Upper Road. Even though in the summer of 1868 the army altered the latter route so that it struck the Pecos thirty-five miles upstream of the bridge, rather than at Horsehead Crossing, the new ford still intimidated and alarmed.[75] Hoping in November to merge the two roads at the Pecos and make one bridge available to both, the army directed new Fort Stockton commander George Gamble to move the bridge upstream to the Upper Road crossing.

Gamble had his command do so immediately, only to find the structure too short to span the Pecos within three or four miles of the new ford. Ordering the bridge returned to its previous location, Gamble wrote Fifth Military District headquarters December 8: "I would state that near Lancaster where the bridge now spans the river, it is of great benefit to both the government and all citizen trains. The ford at this place [Lancaster] being often impassable, any trains were often delayed ten days in crossing."[76]

With the loss of two cavalry companies to Fort Concho in March 1869, Fort Stockton's commander reduced the picket at Lancaster bridge to seven men and, by June, arranged for their bimonthly relief.[77] On June 21, Second Lieutenant G. Valois— marching from Fort Stockton to San Antonio with detachments of companies C and K, Ninth Cavalry—took careful note of the swollen river's effect on the bridge.

"I found the bridge in a dangerous condition, the constant rains having washed away the bank on each side of the stream," he reported.

Although he undertook crude repairs, he feared that the currents would sweep the bridge downstream.

"I therefore respectfully recommend," he said, "that two or three masons with ten or fifteen men and the facilities for hauling material be sent to the place to build a stone foundation which should include the bank on each side of the stream for at least fifteen feet."[78]

Whatever the outcome of his request, Lancaster bridge would not endure. By early 1870, Pontoon Bridge was in place near the Upper Road ford, and the Lancaster bridge fell prey to neglect and the Pecos. On February 13, 1874, Second Lieutenant Thomas C.

Davenport paused a day's march downstream from Lancaster Crossing and made note: "Saw the old bridge which was formerly at the Pecos ford. It is impossible to make any use of it."[79]

Meanwhile, Lancaster Crossing abided. In 1869, W. H. Holmsley's father crossed a cattle herd en route for California along the Texas-California Cattle Trail, which only rarely carried beeves by then.

"He had a full crew of Mexicans and a Negro cook," the younger Holmsley related in 1926. "He was set afoot twice. The cattle got so gentle that they herded afoot to rest their horses up, and the Indians ran in and cut their horses off, thereby setting them afoot. They had to cross one desert driving their cattle afoot. . . . They were about ten months on the trail. I don't think they did much good selling."[80]

With the demise of the bridge and the removal of its outpost, travelers such as the elder Holmsley again looked to Fort Lancaster for escort. On May 10, 1871, officers and fifteen cavalry troopers marched out of Fort Stockton to set up a permanent subpost at the ruins,[81] already the site of a picket. Superiors ordered the men to quarter in tents until huts could be built and set tours of duty at thirty days.

"It is intended that this detachment shall guard the El Paso Road by patrols and scouting parties in the direction of Stockton and east to Howard's Spring . . . ," specified April 27 orders from Department of Texas headquarters. "The detachment will also . . . repair the road from Howard Spring to Fort Stockton, including crossings of any streams [e.g., Lancaster Crossing]."[82]

Despite Fort Lancaster's new designation, relief detachments grew smaller. On January 7, 1872, the withdrawal of two officers and a surgeon reduced the garrison to only eight men: four from the Ninth Cavalry and four from the Twenty-Fourth Infantry.[83]

In 1875, W. R. Owen and a trail boss named Humphries fortunately had no need for escort in driving cattle northwest from Uvalde. "We saw lots of Indian sign but not Indians . . . ," Owen recalled in 1926. "They had been in that country but they never molested us." Fording the Pecos at Lancaster Crossing and bearing upriver, the cowhands kept the cattle on the west bank until Horsehead, where they pushed the drove back to the east side for the long trek upstream to Seven Rivers, New Mexico, and beyond.[84]

As the Indian threat diminished, so, too, did the need for a picket at Fort Lancaster. On January 16, 1880, Burr G. Duval, Murray Harris, and other members of a geological expedition found the post "deserted and in ruins." Wagoning on past free-ranging cattle owned by a rancher named Tarde, they forded Lancaster Crossing, which Duval described as "rapid, though smoothly gliding." Heading upstream, they camped on the Pecos and, in several hours of frivolity, tested the water's worth, as reflected in successive entries in Duval's diary.

The ruins of Fort Lancaster as they appear today. (author)

"Hot discussion tonight . . . as to whether the Pecos water would or would not cook beans. Bet of five dollars. I am referee and am now . . . watching the pot. . . .

"The 'frijoles' have been on nearly two hours, merrily boiling and yet they are as hard as brickbats. . . .

"I am now able to state that Pecos water will not cook beans soft. Boiled them ten hours. They were edible but by no means choice."[85]

There was little reason for levity later that year when floodwaters swept down the Pecos. On September 11, Fort Stockton's commander, Richard F. O'Beirne, reported that "the mail wagon which comes here via Fort Clark has been irregular, being unable at times to cross the Lancaster ford. Nothing has been heard from the subsistence shipped by that route."[86] By September 28, the river had subsided and wagons had resumed crossing.[87]

Although the Texas & Pacific and Southern Pacific railroads helped render the full Texas-California Cattle Trail obsolete in the early 1880s, a few droves continued to raise dust along stretches of the route. In 1884, J. R. Humphries and twelve other men pushed several thousand cattle from South Texas to Fort Sumner, New Mexico, by way of Lancaster Crossing. "From Del Rio to the Pecos one of those many-year droughts had prevailed and there was no water or grass. . . . " Humphries related decades later. "Some suffering was done by both men and cattle, but no complaints."[88]

In 1891, drought also plagued the James Dalrymple drove that set out 2,178-strong from Uvalde for Lancaster Crossing and White Lake, New Mexico. "At this time," recalled drover G. W. Scott, "the range was dry and water scarce, and many of our cattle gave out and had to be left on the trail." Leaving even more to die at Horsehead Crossing, the drovers pushed on, only to lose additional beeves to a sudden chill in the Panhandle. They reached New Mexico with less than half the herd.[89]

Lancaster Crossing vexed not only cattlemen, but also sheepmen such as Jesse M. Kilgore. Driving 330 ewes west for a ranch fifty miles beyond Fort Lancaster in 1893, he and his partners found the Pecos an obstacle unlike any other on the three-month trip.

"We had a hard time crossing the Pecos River," recalled Kilgore. "It sure tries a man's patience to make such an undertaking as we attempted. You can't belong to the church and swim sheep across a stream."

Finally, with the urging of cowboys from the nearby Halff Ranch, the flock negotiated the crossing and pressed on westward.[90]

On into the sunset of the nineteenth century, Lancaster Crossing remained a passageway for emigrants. Westering from Tom Green County in 1896, twenty-eight-year-old William F. Smith forded en route to new beginnings beyond the Pecos.

"He was pulling a horse-powered water well drill," related his son, Olin Smith (born 1917), whose Pecos River ranch of the 1990s extended to within a stone's throw of the crossing. "They came out here homesteading a bunch of land west of Sheffield, and they had to drill wells on it and get it proved out so they could get the title."[91]

By the early 1900s, the straightaway upstream of the ford,

though still without a replacement bridge, nevertheless had regained prominence.

"That's where I went across first time in 1905—I wasn't even a month old," related Edna Brooks, the daughter of homesteader William F. Smith. "There was nothing there except a ferry, a mile above where the new [U.S. Highway 290] bridge is now. That was the only place where you could cross the river at that time. Then we went on [west] to a ranch my daddy had leased between Bakersfield and Fort Stockton."[92]

Within a few years, a successor bridge replaced the ferry,[93] and the old ford of the forty-niners, cattle drovers, stage drivers, and Indian raiders quickly plunged into disuse, destined to be little-known even to a modern West built on its cornerstone. ★

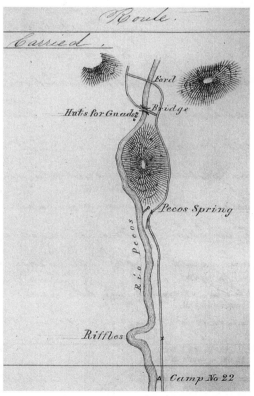

Brevet Lieutenant Colonel Thomas B. Hunt's 1869 map showing Lancaster Crossing, the bridge of 1868, and huts for guards. (National Archives)

Salt Crossing and the old truss bridge as seen today. (author)

⋆ Chapter 8
Other Crossings

Although the aforementioned sites constituted the most significant crossings for travelers in frontier Texas, three other fords in particular, including the earliest known, also gave passage at times.

Salt Crossing

Unlike all other fords on the lower Pecos River, Salt Crossing was a doorway not to the west, but to the northeast, where, four miles away, Juan Cordona Lake[1] offered a white treasure that meant life for early Indians.

Seeking the basin's salt for use as a vital nutrient and as a preservative for meat, the Jumano Indians of the Big Bend—or their prehistoric ancestors—forged a twelve-day footpath northeast to the Pecos. The Salt Trail, as history would know it, struck out from the Rio Grande-Rio Conchos confluence at modern Presidio and bore north along Alamito Creek. Slashing through the Davis Mountains at Paisano Pass, it skirted several springs—Kokernot (near present Alpine), Leoncita, Leon, and Comanche (at modern Fort Stockton)—and pushed down Diamond Y Draw to gravel-bottomed Salt Crossing, five miles east of present Imperial. With Indian acquisition of the horse, travois ruts began to mark the course, and in the late 1700s and early 1800s, the trail deepened under the wooden-wheeled *carretas* (carts) of first Spanish and then Mexican colonists of the Rio Grande-Rio Conchos region.[2]

Rarely used in the mid- and late-1800s and shunned altogether by Fort Stockton patrols in the post-Civil War period,[3] Salt Crossing nevertheless remained a landmark. Sometimes the ford harbored death, as Julius Drew Henderson learned while fighting drought on his father's Davis Mountains ranch in 1887. "A bunch of our cattle had strayed off and tried to go back to Brown County," related Henderson, who was seven in 1887. "They got to the Pecos at Salt Crossing. Twenty head of them went down and drank water and were so weak they could not climb the bank. Some men found them there dead."[4]

With Trans-Pecos ranchers initiating trail drives to the Texas Panhandle in the early 1890s, drovers seeking the most direct route to water holes northeast of the Pecos occasionally pushed herds across Salt Crossing. Among them were B. B. "Ben" Billingsly, who drove six hundred steers to the Panhandle from the Davis Mountains.[5]

Although Salt Crossing and its downstream counterpart, Horsehead Crossing, lay only eighteen river miles apart, they were the only points in the vicinity where the Pecos's sharp banks yielded. As young men, Julius Henderson, Clay McGonagill, Nallie Graham, and George Lee seized upon that knowledge in their quest for Pecos mustangs.

"There was two bunches of ponies that ranged in that country," related Henderson decades later. "Some were light bays and very small; the others were dark bays, bull-faced, and stocking-footed. . . . We did what was known as walking those ponies down. There was only two waterings on the Pecos down there, Horsehead and Salt Crossing. They put a man at each place to keep those horses away from the water. We had some saddle horses that liked to run horses. We rode those at night and followed those horses day and night and gave them no time to eat or get water. In about four days, they were about . . . given out. We threw our saddle horses in with them and drove them east . . . . We had about twenty-five head of them."

Already exhausted, the mustangs struggled in the ensuing sands, forcing the young cowboys to hobble five of the animals and push on without them for a pen and a water well. Reaching the corral with about twenty head, the cowhands were disheartened to realize the ordeal had rendered the mustangs virtually worthless.

"We were sure sick," said Henderson, "but we went back to get those we had left hobbled and found every one of them dead. When we got back to the pen, about half of those were dead. We opened the gate and let them go and called it a day."[6]

In the 1910s, engineers spanned the Pecos with a bridge in the immediate vicinity of Salt Crossing, the exact location of which is a matter of contention today.[7]

"There may be more than one Salt Crossing . . . ," observed I. C. "Tiny" Earp, whose ranch of the 1990s included the bridge site. "That old river shifted and changed back in that day and time. . . . Flood conditions would wash one crossing out and . . . if it deposited gravel in certain areas, which it quite often did, why, they'd pick up another crossing."

Drawing from information that pioneers had passed along to him, Earp, who was born in 1926, pinpointed three possible sites for Salt Crossing: at the old truss bridge of the 1910s; ten river miles upstream where the Pecos makes its first bend after flowing under the FM Road 1053 bridge; and an undetermined distance (within three-quarters of a mile, said one source) downstream from the bridge of the 1910s.[8]

Billy Rankin, who began ranching along the Pecos three miles below Horsehad Crossing in 1928, suggested a point a few hundred yards downstream of the old structure for Salt Crossing. "There's a good gravel crossing; it got called the Gravel Crossing . . . ," he observed. "You could get across it [with] stock. [It had] good gravel on both sides and across the bottom."

Though lost in time and myriad salt cedars, Salt Crossing nevertheless stands alone as a ford that spanned centuries of Pecos River history.

Adobe Crossing

Although without the rich history of Horsehead Crossing, Adobe Crossing nevertheless shares a distinction with it—both fords found their way onto U. S. Geological Survey topographic maps while other frontier Pecos River crossings slipped into cartographic oblivion.

Nevertheless, Adobe's history is obscure. Cliff Newland, who was born in 1886, remembered Adobe as one of "only three crossings that was popular when I was a kid."[10] Situated southeast of present Girvin and three and one-half miles below the U.S. Highway 67 river bridge,[11] Adobe lay midway between Horsehead and Pontoon Bridge—the two other popular crossings of Newland's youth.

Although Fort Stockton records (which extend through 1886) make no mention of Adobe Crossing,[12] post correspondence and Pecos folklore suggest a Mormon, Chinese, or Mexican origin. Researcher W. R. Baggett related in 1942 that "we had been told that the Mormons put in a colony somewhere in that Pecos Valley country and later abandoned it and moved in to the State of Sonora, Mexico." Arthur Young, who ranched the old Torres Irrigation and Manufacturing Company farm on the Pecos in the 1880s, recalled in the early 1940s that "the place known as the Mormon settlement was on the east side of the river and was also called the 'Adobe Walls' and 'Chinese Reservation.'" The latter designation holds the hint that Chinese laborers colonized the site after completing the Texas & Pacific or Southern Pacific railroads.

Young reported that the Mormon operation included a dam ten to fifteen miles upstream from Spanish Dam, a distance which would have placed it near Adobe Crossing. He further related that when he first visited the settlement ruins in 1883, he found a roofless house surrounded by an adobe or rock fence.[13]

In April 1878, when the Torres farm was still in operation, Second Lieutenant John Bigelow, Jr., of Fort Stockton scouted upstream from the fields and described a site he termed "Adobe Walls," approximately one mile east of a Pecos tributary with a "good water hole."[14] Fort Stockton Lieutenant W. H. Beck, en route up the river's west bank to Horsehead the following July, found "the bottom between Pecos [Pontoon] Bridge and Adobe Walls almost entirely under water, and it was with the steadiest pulling that the wagon reached the dam on the Pecos [Spanish Dam], about eight miles above Torres Ranche, by sundown."[15] A field map sketched by Second Lieutenant C. Esterly of Fort Stockton in October 1878 further documents the existence of Adobe Walls upstream of the point where the El Paso-to-San Antonio road struck the Pecos.[16]

On January 18, 1880, Burr G. Duval and his geological expedition—headed west along the Lower Road—marched up the Pecos and camped at "Doby Walls." In his log, he described it as a "Mexican settlement" and a "Mexican hacienda and cultivated fields." Although he may have been referring specifically to the Torres farm headquarters, he added that "there is quite a Mexican settlement up and down the Pecos here."[17]

Although the proximity of Adobe Crossing to Adobe Walls—and the similarity in their names—suggest a related origin, it is also possible that travelers dubbed the ford "Adobe" simply for descriptive reasons.

"I imagine the Adobe Crossing got it[s] [name] because there wasn't no quicksand there," observed Cliff Newland, who remembered his employer, James Currie, frequently crossing by buckboard at the site. "It was a hard bottom [like adobe brick]. I don't know that it's rock—there's some rock—but anyway, it's a hard bottom, might've been hard dirt, and they called it Adobe Crossing. . . . But generally the water was deeper there usually than any . . . of them other crossings."[18]

As a boy, Roy McDonald (who was born in 1906) frequently crossed the Pecos at a ford that in all likelihood was Adobe Crossing. "[It was] the best crossing in this country," McDonald observed in 1982. "That was on the old road that come from San Angelo down to old Adams post office and went on into Fort Stockton. It was almost solid-rock bottomed and there was water boiling up [from] a spring right out in the middle of the river."

McDonald recalled that freight wagons, each with as many as seven trailers, sometimes would cross at the site.

"They had a barrel on each side of them ol' wagons," he said. "They'd stop right in the middle of that river and [the freighters] had a big ol' bucket with a rope on it, and they'd dip that water up, clean, out of that spring and fill them barrels."[19]

Roy McDonald in 1982. (author)

Twenty-five-year-old Billy Rankin, pushincattle upstream from the Cap Yates spread to the old Tol Dawson Ranch below Horsehead in 1931, struck the west bank of the Pecos between Spanish Dam and Girvin—apparently at Adobe Crossing.

"There was a crossing—not a very good one," he related. "I crossed a little bunch of yearlings there, about sixty or seventy."[20]

In that same year, Nora Locklin and her husband, Dee, took up a twenty-section ranch that included Adobe Crossing. "We have crossed that, my husband and I," Mrs. Locklin recalled six decades later. "Sometimes you could take a pickup across if it was low. There wasn't much wood [for heating and cooking] on the east side of the river where we were, so we went across to get wood. It was just hard dirt. See, the Pecos River had quicksand in it then and it [Adobe] was tested; it had no quicksand. And the banks were flat, more than other places."

Nevertheless, the ford was miry enough to trouble the Locklins' sheep. "They'd get out in the crossing and bog down," she remembered. "It was like an adobe bottom: as long as you moved fast, took quick steps, you were all right, but if you slowed up you'd bog down. And sometimes they'd have to rope the sheep and drag them out."

Despite Adobe's pitfalls, she said, the ford "was known for miles around as a place you could get across. It was still in use when we left in '41; they crossed cattle."[21]

Regional cattle drives soon faded into memory, and Adobe Crossing fell victim to a changing Pecos and myriad salt cedars.

S Crossing

Where automobile tires now sing across a Pecos River bridge at high speed, wagon wheels once creaked down the sloped banks of a gravelly ford.

S Crossing, situated adjacent to the Texas Highway 349 bridge[22] eight miles northwest of present Iraan, is unique among lower Pecos fords, for it alone marks the course of a modern thoroughfare and thereby spans the gulf between wagon travel and state-of-the-art motoring. Nevertheless, travelers of the 1870s first coveted it not as a crossing, but rather as a watering place for draft animals and saddle stock frustrated by the river's generally sheer banks.

Marching from Fort Stockton to the Pecos in February 1874,

S Crossing as seen today. (author)

Second Lieutenant Thomas C. Davenport and a detachment from Company M, Ninth Cavalry, kept a sharp lookout along the Lower Road for just such a break in the barrier banks. Pushing downstream from Pontoon Bridge, they found it at the two-mile mark—a distance that placed them at the exact later site of S Crossing, according to U.S. Army measurements eleven years later.

"Two miles below the new station [Camp Melvin] the animals can be watered very easily on the right [west] bank," Davenport noted in his log on February 7. Surveying the surrounding terrain, he added, "No trees of any kind. Hills covered with rocks—limestone. Grass very poor."[23]

It is unclear whether prior travelers already had made use of the watering place, but succeeding parties soon did so, though not always peacefully. On June 4, 1874, First Lieutenant B. Dawson of Fort Stockton and a Ninth Cavalry detachment camped "about two miles below Camp Melvin" and described it as "the place where Mr.

Thomas had his horses run off by Indians." Dawson reported the grass "poor" at the site and the Pecos "very high, running with its bank and very muddy."[24]

Within a few years, animals no longer merely watered at the gentle banks—they splashed across with riders astride or wagons in tow. The crossing likely was already in use when twenty-two-year-old W. H. Holmsley rode up in 1882 and signed on with a cow outfit run by Nub Pulliam of San Angelo.

"Pulliam owned the SSS brand (three S)," Holmsley recalled in 1926. "He held range [on the river's west side] from about seven or eight miles below old Fort Lancaster up to Horsehead Crossing. . . . M. [Myer] Halff and brother owned the range on the east. . . . Pulliam once owned a strip from about the fort [Lancaster] up to Pontoon Crossing. . . . Below the Pontoon Crossing was one called the Old S Crossing for our ranch."[25]

The march of Captain George W. Wedemeyer and Company F, Sixteenth Infantry, from Fort Stockton to Fort Concho in 1885 signaled military use of S Crossing. "Marched down the river two miles below old Pontoon Crossing to the ford [S Crossing] . . . ," Wedemeyer wrote in his diary on May 24. "Mounted men rode at the head of the teams to keep them from going down stream with the strong current."

Immediately across the Pecos they camped, remaining until early the next afternoon so the saddle stock could water in preparation for the long, dry march to the Middle Concho River.[26]

In the fall of 1885, F. S. Millard crossed the Pecos, likely at S Crossing, en route to a Trans-Pecos ranch. "We got [with]in fifty yards of the river before we could see any sign of it," he recalled. "We had to swim the river, it was always swimming then."[27]

Sometimes, even the proximity of S Crossing's ample waters was not enough to save animals from perishing of thirst. In the 1880s, J. D. Slaughter came upon hundreds of cattle carcasses—all bearing the Long S brand—on the rim of the east-side bluff sentineling the crossing. Unable to catch the scent of water below, the thirst-maddened beeves had refused to descend, despite desperate measures by their drovers.[28]

Even harsher judgment awaited cattlemen in the fall of 1885, when a drought took hold and began to choke the Pecos and its budding ranching industry.

"Lee Heard and Tom White . . . each had a little bunch [of

cattle] and ran them on Pulliam's range . . . ," related Holmsley, who grazed 350 of his own beeves at Pulliam's S Crossing ranch in 1886. "There was a drouth during the years 1885, 1886, and 1887, and you could walk on dead cattle by that time. I didn't have over twenty-five head when it was over. Pulliam's stock were native cattle, and didn't die so badly.

"I drove to [San] Angelo with herd after herd from the Pecos, without water on the way from the Pecos to the [Middle] Concho. We never would lose stout cattle. We drove from Pontoon Crossing . . . across to the Concho. It was about eighty miles, and would take us about three days."[29]

Sometime before 1904, rancher Tom Hickox gained control of forty sections of land along the lower Pecos. "It extended to S Crossing . . . just above S Water Hole . . . ," said his daughter Opal Nix, who recalled that Hickox altered the ford's banks to ease the burden on wagons. "He took his scrapers and his Mexicans and mules, and scooped off both edges because there was no quicksand there."[30]

On into the 1920s, wagon wheels still rutted S Crossing's banks. "We crossed there in a wagon . . .[with] a team of mares . . . two or three times about 1925 . . . ," recalled Paul Patterson in 1993. "The banks just kind of sloped off nicely. Say you were going south[west]—you'd go in and then go down the river maybe ten yards or fifteen yards and come out on another gentle bank. . . . [The water] was about a foot and a half [deep], and on dry years maybe not that much. . . . It had a good, solid, rock bottom—it never did get boggy. . . . As well as I remember, there wasn't much brush there."

Upon acquiring a Model T Ford truck later in the 1920s, Patterson sometimes hauled wool, mohair, or cottonseed cake across the ford. He recalled: "That old truck couldn't pull the hat off your head. . . . Sometimes we've have to unload some of our wool or cake to cross the river and then go back and pick up the rest of it. . . . The north[east] bank might've been a little steeper than the other one, because we'd always have trouble going that way . . . more than the other."

In 1931 or 1932, a chance meeting with an elderly man at S Crossing gave Patterson insight into Indian life at the location. Related Patterson:

"We stopped there at S Crossing . . . and this old man was coming through there and he said, 'I was here, right here, fifty-five years ago today and . . . there was some Indians camped off over here—they weren't hostile or anything, just sort of poor, raggedy. They weren't on the war path, because they didn't have anything to fight with.' He said he was working for some big cow outfit [at the time]."

Working cattle himself on an adjacent ranch in 1934, Patterson turned his horse into the river about two hundred yards upstream of the crossing and found dramatic reason to appreciate the ford's firm footing.

"I was just going out in there to see if he wanted a drink of water . . . ," he recalled. "There was big old rocks [below the bank]. . . . I thought, well, where there's big old rocks laying, it's bound to be solid ground. Just about two feet [out], my horse bogged plum' up to his belly and we scrambled around. I didn't get out any further. It had come such a rise that those rocks had settled on top of that mud."[31]

Once an important point on an Old West trail of dust, S Crossing long since has lapsed into oblivion along a New West trail of asphalt.

Obscure Crossings

Additional crossings mentioned in Fort Stockton records of the 1870s or in oral recollections of the region's pioneers include:

— Narbo's Crossing, presumably where northwest-trending Narrow Bow Draw strikes the Pecos ten-and-a-half miles southeast of present Orla. Variant spellings include Narboe's, Narbow, and Marboe's. Situated about twelve miles below Sand Bend and at the upper end of the big flat in which the old Hashknife outfit headquarters lay, Narbo's originated as a wagon crossing prior to 1868. "There was an emigrant train on its way to California which struck the river there," said pioneer Pecos cattleman James P. Jones in 1927. "A man by that name got out in the river, waded and swam around, and found a suitable crossing." J. K. Millwee, who crossed 1,200 head of cattle at Narbo's in an 1868 drive up the Goodnight-Loving Trail, agreed that this "dandy" ford and "good watering" spot began as a wagon crossing. However, Millwee believed it to be named for cattle drover Pete Narbo of Weatherford, who drove up the trail in 1867 and presumably crossed his herd en route to Fort Sumner. At any rate, by the fall of 1880, ranchers Narbo and Gibson grazed 4,000 head of cattle on the Pecos, possibly near the crossing.

— Pecos Falls Crossing, evidently the "Great Falls" that marked the point where the eventual Reeves-Pecos county line would intersect the river.

— Frazier's (or Frazer's) Crossing, three and one-half miles by wagon road below Pecos Falls.

— Hackberry Crossing, thirty miles by wagon road above Horsehead Crossing.

— Mosely (or Moseley) Crossing, downstream from Horsehead Crossing.

— Sixmile Crossing, where Sixmile Draw strikes the Pecos six miles north of Sheffield.

— Fourmile Crossing, where Fourmile Draw intersects the river four miles north of Sheffield.[32]

The natural "state of Texas" rock sentineling the Pecos near Four Mile Crossing. (author)

Horsehead Crossing as it appears today. (author)

On May 28, 1923, Santa Rita #1 blew in near Texon twenty-eight miles northeast of the Pecos and ushered in the West Texas oil boom.[1] The consequences for the river were not all good. In 1931 Dee and Nora Locklin, crossing a cattle herd below old Pontoon Crossing, lost six cows to an oil slick in the river.[2]

For decades already, the river's water quality had been in question. Occasionally, travelers had found it palatable, but more often than not, they had agreed with Zenas Bliss, who in 1886 had termed it "the worst of any stream I have ever seen."[3] But just one year after the Locklins' misfortune, a study by the Bureau of Economic Geology broadened Bliss's scope to the ultimate. Highly impregnated with minerals and ten times saltier than the sea, the Pecos carried the "world's worst" water, said Dr. C. L. Baker.[4]

As early as July 1890, dams at present Carlsbad in southern New Mexico impeded the Pecos, and the irrigated croplands that thrived on into twentieth-century Texas depleted its waters more. In 1936, Red Bluff Dam impounded water just south of the Texas-New Mexico line and further choked this once-wild river.[5] By 1964, Cliff Newland rightfully could liken the Pecos to an "irrigatin' ditch" and lament, "[If] a man seen that river fifty years ago, and see it now, you couldn't make him believe it was the Pecos River."[6]

Then, in 1968, the completion of Amistad Reservoir on the Rio Grande killed the last several miles of free-flowing Pecos and inundated many of the rockshelters of the river's earliest inhabitants.[7] By the approach of the twenty-first century, additional impounding in New Mexico further threatened the Texas coils, reducing the river in places to a polluted trickle through a tangle of salt cedars that lined banks sloughed and forgotten.

Today, except for brief, unyielding rapids in its spring-fed lower canyons, the Rio Pecos of Texas is a river tamed, even dying. Yet its frontier crossings, immersed more in myth and history than in water, seem fated to live forever in Old West romance. ★

Born in 1951, Patrick Dearen grew up in Sterling City, Texas, and earned a journalism degree from the University of Texas at Austin. A former award-winning reporter for two West Texas daily newspapers, he is the author of six other books, including a novel, *When Cowboys Die*, a finalist for the Spur Award of Western Writers of America. He has written two previous books of Pecos country lore and legend—*Castle Gap and the Pecos Frontier* and *Portraits of the Pecos Frontier*. He also scripted and co-produced the documentary video *Graveyard of the West: The Pecos River of Texas Where Myth Meets History*. In addition to searching the Pecos for signs of its frontier crossings, he has backpacked the river's headwaters, canoed its lower canyons, and hiked the old wagon road and cattle trail from Horsehead Crossing to Castle Gap. He lives in Midland, Texas, with his wife Mary and son Wesley. ★

Patrick Dearon mid-stream at Fourmile Crossing on the Pecos

Unless otherwise indicated, all towns, counties, and map quadrangles are in Texas.

Chapter 1 • River of the West

1. Harry J. Shafer, *Ancient Texans: Rock Art and Lifeways Along the Lower Pecos* (Houston: Gulf Publishing Company for Witte Museum of the San Antonio Museum Association, 1986), 37.

2. The river's length, presumably including all bends, is from Delmar Hayter, "The Crookedest River in the World: A Social and Economic Development of the Pecos River Valley from 1878 to 1950," (dissertation, 1988), 11, Southwest Collection, Texas Tech University, Lubbock, Texas (hereinafter, Southwest Collection).

3. This discussion of early peoples on the Pecos is primarily from Shafer, *Ancient Texans*, 58, 59, 61, 63, 65, 67, 69, 102, 104. For representative photos of rock art in the lower canyons, see Jim Zintgraff (photography) and Solveig A. Turpin (text), *Pecos River Rock Art* (San Antonio: Sandy McPherson Publishing Company, 1991). Information on Midland Man is from Dr. Fred Wendorf, telephone interview with author, Dallas, fall 1982; and Dr. Fred Wendorf, taped telephone interview with author, Dallas, 10 June 1991. Wendorf was the original investigating archaeologist. For a discussion on Midland Man, see Patrick Dearen, *Portraits of the Pecos Frontier* (Lubbock: Texas Tech University Press, 1993), 100-105.

4. See the discussion on Salt Crossing in Chapter 8.

5. Diary of the expedition of John Pope, *Reports of Explorations and Surveys to Ascertain the Most Practicable and Economical Route for a Railroad from the Mississippi River to the Pacific Ocean*. Vol. II, 33rd Cong., 2nd sess., House of Representatives Executive Document No. 91 (Washington: 1855), 60.

6. Journal of Juan Dominguez de Mendoza in Herbert Eugene Bolton, *Spanish Exploration in the Southwest* (New York: Barnes and Noble, Inc., reprint, 1952), 329, 339, 343.

7. Narrative of Espejo in Bolton, *Spanish Exploration*, 189-190. For information on Juan Cordona Lake (situated in present Crane County), see Patrick Dearen, *Castle Gap and the Pecos Frontier* (Fort Worth: Texas Christian University Press, 1988), 63-84.

8. W. W. Newcomb, Jr., *The Indians of Texas* (Austin: University of Texas Press, 1961; reprint 1969), 23-24, 226-231, 238-239.

9. "Narrative of Cabeza de Vaca" in *Spanish Explorers in the Southern United States 1528-1543* (Austin: Texas State Historical Association, 1984), 98-99.

10. Narrative of Espejo in Bolton, *Spanish Exploration*, 189-190. Cicuye was near present Pecos, New Mexico.

11. Victor J. Smith, "Early Spanish Exploration in the Big Bend of Texas," *West Texas Historical and Scientific Society* 2 (1928), 58.

12. J. Frank Dobie, "Cabeza de Vaca and Horsehead," *The New Texas Reader* (San Antonio: Naylor Company, 1947), 49.

13. "Account of the Discovery of the Buffalo, 1599," in Bolton, *Spanish Exploration*, 223.

14. Newcomb, *Indians*, 86-88, 107-109, 114, 156-157, 161 (map), 233; Ernest Wallace and E. Adamson Hoebel, *The Comanches: Lords of the South Plains* (Norman: University of Oklahoma Press, 1986), 12, 38, 39, 288, 289; and O. W. Williams, *Pioneer Surveyor-Frontier Lawyer: The Personal Narrative of O. W. Williams, 1877-1902*, ed. by S. D. Myres (El Paso: Texas Western College Press, 1966), 278.

15. "A History of Texas," *Texas Almanac 1970-71* (A. H. Belo Corporation, 1969), 79, 83, 87.

16. Dearen, *Castle Gap*, 66-68.

17. See Dearen, *Castle Gap*, 69-70; Mabelle Eppard Martin, "California Emigrant Roads Through Texas," *The Southwestern Historical Quarterly* (hereinafter *SHQ*) 28, No. 4 (April 1925), 287-301; and A. B. Bender, "Opening Routes Across West Texas, 1848-1850," *SHQ* 37, No. 2 (October 1933), 116-135. While I chose to give distances in air miles in this discussion, elsewhere in this volume I sometimes elected to give distances in wagon miles. Neither method accurately reflects river miles.

18. Barry Scobee, *Old Fort Davis* (San Antonio: Naylor Company, 1947), 11.

19. Department of Texas Special Order No. 79, 20 July 1855, RG 94, National Archives; post returns, August 1855, Fort Lancaster, Texas, National Archives, microfilm in my possession.

20. Clayton Williams, *Texas' Last Frontier: Fort Stockton and the Trans-Pecos 1861-1895* (College Station: Texas A&M University Press, 1982), 64.

21. Special Order No. 32 from headquarters, Department of Texas, San Antonio, Texas, 24 February 1861, in *The War of the Rebellion: A Compilation of the Official Records of the Union and Confederate Armies* (Washington: Government Printing Office, 1880-1901, reprint edition by National Historical Society, Gettysburg, 1972), series 1, 1: 594 (hereinafter *The War of the Rebellion*). Date of the Texas vote for secession is from Mary G. Crawford, "A History of West Texas," *1990-91 Texas Almanac* (Dallas: The Dallas Morning News, 1989), 43.

22. *Waco Register*, 21 April 1866, as cited in Crawford, "A History of West Texas," 44.

23. *The Texas Almanac for 1867* (Galveston: The Galveston News), 197.

24. "The Cattle Movement," *Texas Live Stock Journal*, 5 December 1885, 2.

25. Post returns, July 1867, Fort Stockton, microfilm, Southwest Collection.

26. Crawford, "A History of West Texas," 47.

27. Joe S. McCombs in Ben O. Grant and J. R. Webb, "On the Cattle Trail and Buffalo Range, Joe S. McCombs," *West Texas Historical Association Year Book* (hereinafter WTHA Year Book) 2 (November 1935), 100. For information on Mustang Springs, situated near present Stanton, see Dearen, *Portraits*, 106-114.

28. Paul Patterson, "A Forgotten Empire of the Pecos," *The Cattleman* (May 1943), 24-25.

29. The once-thriving breadbasket along the Pecos is now largely a wasteland, due to irrigated water "salting-up" the ground and the failure of farmers to rotate crops (Bill Leftwich, taped interview with Mike Cox, Fort Davis, Texas, fall 1991, copy in my possession).

30. F. S. Millard, *A Cowpuncher of the Pecos* (J. Marvin Hunter, n. d.), 36. Throughout this discussion, I have edited Millard's comments for spelling and punctuation.

31. Cliff Newland, taped interview with Elmer Kelton, Upton County, 23 August 1964, in possession of author.

32. Barney Hubbs, videotaped interview with Mike Cox, Pecos, 21 October 1991, in my possession.

33. Jim Witt, taped telephone interview with author, Loving, New Mexico, 17 July 1993.

34. Hubbs, interview with Cox.

35. James F. Hinkle, *Early Days of a Cowboy on the Pecos* (Santa Fe: Stagecoach Press, reprint 1965), 44. Hinkle cowboyed on the Pecos in southern New Mexico in the 1880s.

36. Millard, *Cowpuncher*, 36.

37. Sergeant L. B. Caruthers, Company E, Frontier Battalion, to Lieutenant C. L. Nevill, commanding Company E, Frontier Battalion, 8 June 1880, copy of letter, Clayton Wheat Williams Collection, Nita Stewart Haley Memorial Library, Midland (hereinafter Williams Collection, Haley Library).

38. As buffalo hunters considered it. See J. Frank Dobie, *A Vaquero of the Brush Country* (New York: Grosset and Dunlap Publishers, reprint, n. d.), 274.

39. Ramon F. Adams, *Western Words: A Dictionary of the American West* (Norman: University of Oklahoma Press, rev. edition, 1968), 223.

40. Paul Patterson, videotaped interview with author, Crane, 29 April 1991; and Dobie, *Vaquero*, 275. Throughout this volume, I have used the verb *pecos* in a broader sense to include any murder committed along the Pecos.

41. This discussion on the Big Drift is based on: Betty Orbeck, ed., "Walter C. Cochran's Memoirs of Early Day Cattlemen," *The Texas Permian Historical Annual* 1, No. 1 (August 1961), 38; *Fort Worth Gazette*, 16 January 1885; D. H. McNairy, interview by J. Evetts Haley (hereinafter Haley), Mineral Wells, 22 January 1932, typescript, Haley Library; H. D. Beal, interview by Haley, Gail, 11 September 1931, typescript in Haley Library; W. H. Holmsley, interview by Haley, 17 October 1926, in "South Plains Interviews," Haley Library; and Lod Calohan, interview by Haley, Kansas City, Missouri, 1 January 1926, in "South Plains Interviews," Haley Library.

42. Orbeck, "Cochran's Memoirs," 38.

43. This discussion on the drought of 1885-1887 is based on: "Texas Cattle Losses," *Rocky Mountain News*, Denver, Colorado, 29 January 1886; "Thousands of Cattle Dying," *Globe Livestock Journal*, Dodge City, Kansas, 25 May 1886; "From El Paso," (letter to the editor) *Texas Live Stock Journal*, 29 May 1886; Millard, *Cowpuncher*, 40; "Stockings," *Globe Livestock Journal*, Dodge City, Kansas, 27 April

1886; and Orbeck, "Cochran's Memoirs," 41.

44. "1933 Driest Year Save One Since Rain Records Have Been Kept in Reeves County," *The Pecos Enterprise and Gusher*, 27 July 1934.

45. Billy Rankin, taped interview with author, Rankin, 9 August 1989.

46. L. B. Eddins, taped interview with author, Kermit, 5 September 1989. Eddins cowboyed on a Pecos River ranch during the drought.

47. Hallie Stillwell, taped telephone interview with author, Brewster County, 10 July 1993.

Chapter 2 • Pope's Crossing

1. This description of Pope's Crossing and its surroundings is based on: Captain John Pope, "Sketch Exhibiting newly Discovered Springs. Accompanying a Letter dated June 4th, 1858. Submitted with annual report from Office Ex. & Sur., War Dept.," Senate Executive Document No. 1, House Executive Document No. 2, 35th Cong., 2nd sess.; U.S. Geological Survey, Red Bluff Quadrangle, 7.5-minute series (topographic map); Haley, interview with author, Midland, 4 November 1993; W. R. "Jake" Owen, interview with Haley, Carlsbad, New Mexico, 24 June 1937, Haley Library; Norman Eisenwine, taped interview with author, Pecos, 1 July 1993; and Roscoe P. Conkling and Margaret B. Conkling, *The Butterfield Overland Mail*, 1857-1869, Vol. 1 (Glendale: Arthur H. Clark Company, 1947), 374, 386.

2. Alton Hughes, *Pecos: A History of the Pioneer West* (Seagraves: Pioneer Book Publishers, 1978), 7.

3. Haley, interview, 4 November 1993; Haley, *Rough Times—Tough Fiber* (Canyon: Palo Duro Press, 1976), 149 (photo).

4. Clay Slack, taped interview with Paul Patterson, 5 July 1968, Pecos, Southwest Collection.

5. Haley, *Rough Times*, 149.

6. Diary of the expedition of John Pope, 59-60; and U.S. Geological Survey, Red Bluff Quadrangle, (Eddy County) New Mexico, 7.5-minute series (topographic map).

7. Lee Myers, "Pope's Wells," *New Mexico Historical Review* 38, No. 4, (October 1963), 275.

8. Myers, "Pope's Wells," 279 (quotation from Pope's report).

9. Ibid., 282, 283, 284-295.

10. Grace Thormann King, "Captain John Pope, First Driller in the Permian Basin," *The Texas Permian Historical Annual* 2, No. 1 (August 1962), 17.

11. Pope, "Sketch Exhibiting newly Discovered Springs."

12. Haley, composite of statements made in taped telephone interview with author, Midland, 7 October 1992; and interview, 4 November 1993. Information on Haley's age upon first lodging at the site is from Haley, *Rough Times*, 151.

13. Slack, interview with Patterson.

14. Uncredited letter, presumably written by John Pope, *The Washington Union* (Washington City), Vol. 14, No. 153 (12 October 1858, 2, col. 4), in archives, Permian Basin Petroleum Museum, Library, and Hall of Fame, Midland.

15. Conkling and Conkling, *Butterfield*, Vol. 1, 385.

16. Waterman Ormsby, *The Butterfield Overland Mail* (San Marino: Huntington Library, 1955), 68, 69-72. Information about the topography between Pope's Camp and the ford is from Conkling and Conkling, Butterfield, Vol. 1, 386.

17. J. W. Williams, *Old Texas Trails* (Burnet: Eakin Press, 1979), 365.

18. Conkling and Conkling, *Butterfield*, Vol. 1, 375.

19. John P. Wilson, *Fort Sumner, New Mexico* (Santa Fe: Museum of New Mexico, 1974), 4.

20. *Charles Goodnight*, "Recollections II," 70-71, typescript, Haley Library.

21. Ibid., 71-72.

22. Ibid., 71.

23. Brevet Major General Griffin to commanding officer, 27 July 1867, letters and telegrams received, microfilm, Fort Stockton Public Library, Fort Stockton (hereinafter Fort Stockton).

24. Haley, *Charles Goodnight: Cowman and Plainsman* (Norman and London: University of Oklahoma Press, 1987), 169-183; J. Marvin Hunter, compiler and ed., *The Trail Drivers of Texas* (Austin: University of Texas Press, reprint, 1985), 903-913; and Grace Miller White, "Oliver Loving, the First Trail Driver," *Frontier Times* 19, No. 7 (April 1942), 273-275.

25. Captain George Gamble to Lieutenant J. S. Loud, post adjutant, 4 October 1867, letters and telegrams received, Fort Stockton.

26. Maria Shrode journal in Sandra L. Myres, ed., *Ho for California! Women's Overland Diaries from the Huntington Library* (San Marino: Huntington Library, 1980), 269, 270, 271, 272, 276.

27. George Owens, interview with Haley, Pecos, 10 January 1927, in "Notes Upon the Ranches of the Pecos and Trans-Pecos," Haley Library.

28. Captain E. G. Bush to assistant adjutant (hereinafter AA) general, Department of Texas, 2 October 1873, letters and telegrams sent, Fort Stockton; and "Journal of march of Company D, 9th Cavalry, commanded by Captain F. S. Dodge, 9th Cavalry, from Fort Stockton, Texas and return, pursuant to special order number 13 . . . September 3, 1873" and accompanying "map of route, Company D, 9th Cavalry, from September 3 to September 12, 1873," journal of marches, scouts, and expeditions, Fort Stockton. Great Falls was situated where the present Reeves-Pecos county line strikes the Pecos.

29. Bush to AA general, 2 October 1873; and "Journal of the march of detachment of fifteen men of Company D, 9th U.S. Cavalry, from Fort Stockton, Texas to Pope's Crossing, Pecos River, Texas, via Horsehead Crossing, and return, pursuant to special orders number 68 dated . . . Fort Stockton, Texas, October 4, 1873," journal of marches, scouts, and expeditions, Fort Stockton.

30. Crawford, "A History of West Texas," 47.

31. James P. Jones, interview with Haley, Rocky Arroyo, New Mexico, 13-14 January 1927, in "Notes on the History of Southeastern New Mexico," Haley Library.

32. Hunter, *Trail Drivers*, 977-984.

33. Colonel George A. Armes to AA general, Department of Texas, 8 September 1879, journal of marches, scouts, and expeditions, Fort Stockton.

34. Colonel George A. Armes, *Ups and Downs of an Army Officer* (Washington: 1900), 464; and Armes to AA general, 8 September 1879.

35. Second Lieutenant John Bigelow to adjutant general, 9 December 1879, journal of marches, scouts, and expeditions, Fort Stockton.

36. Caruthers to Nevill, 8 June 1880.

37. Lily Klasner, *My Girlhood Among Outlaws* (Tucson: University of Arizona Press, 1972), 27-30. Lily also reported finding at Horsehead a fresh grave marked with a wagon endgate bearing a girl's name and age. Lily's brother, Robert Adam Casey, said their trip came in the winter of 1868-1869. (Casey, interview with J. Evetts Haley, Picacho, New Mexico, 25 June 1937, Haley Library.)

38. Captain George Gamble to Lieutenant C. E. Morse, acting assistant adjutant (hereinafter AAA) general, 31 August 1868, letters and telegrams sent, Fort Stockton.

39. W. S. Wheeland, "A Buried Treasure: A Tragedy of the Pecos River, as Told by an Old Timer," (letter to the editor), the *Eddy* (New Mexico) *Argus*, 30 April 1892.

40. Ed Gregory to commanding officer, Fort Stockton, 18 December 1872, letters and telegrams received, Fort Stockton. Situated along the road extending west from Horsehead, Agua Bonita (or Antelope Spring) lay twelve miles northeast of Fort Stockton. See Clayton Williams, *Last Frontier*, 133.

41. James Trainer, post trader and army contractor, to commanding officer, Fort Stockton, 30 December 1872, letters and telegrams received, Fort Stockton.

42. Second Lieutenant John Conline to post adjutant, 5 January 1873, letters and telegrams received, Fort Stockton.

43. Cora Melton Cross, "Breaking a Stampede of 10,000 Buffalo," *Frontier Times* 6, No. 7 (April 1929), 274-275. This article, based on the recollections of Cantrell, does not specify the ford where the drovers found the grave. Although it is possible the grave lay at another ford, the fact that they were pushing a herd up the Pecos suggests Pope's Crossing, the preferred crossing point on the Goodnight-Loving Trail.

44. Slack, interview with Patterson.

45. This study of Robert Olinger is based on: Robert M. Utley, *Billy the Kid: A Short and Violent Life* (Lincoln: University of Nebraska Press, 1989), 135, 149-151, 176-181; A. T. Windham, interview with Haley, Pecos, 10 January 1927, in "Notes Upon the Ranches of the Pecos and Trans-Pecos, 1927-1928," Haley Library; Charles Ballard, interview with Haley and Hervey Chesley, Luna, New Mexico, 9 June 1939, Haley Library; W. Wier, interview with Haley, Monument, New Mexico, 22 June 1937, Haley Library; Cline, *Alias Billy the Kid*, 104-109; Bill O'Neal, *Encyclopedia of Western Gunfighters* (Norman: University of Oklahoma Press, 1979), 246-247; W. R. Owen, interview with Haley, 2 March 1933, Carlsbad, New Mexico, Haley Library; W. R. Owen, interview with Haley, 24 June 1937; and Klasner, *My Girlhood Among Outlaws*, 187-188.

Olinger confidante Lily Klasner, defending Olinger decades later as "considerate and generous," seemed to imply that the shooting victim at Pope's was John Jones, against whom Olinger had harbored a grudge for slaying John Beckwith at Seven Rivers in 1879. Holding to Olinger's version of the Jones killing, Lily claimed that he fired in self-defense, after Jones's rifle shot had missed Olinger at close range. W. R. Owen, however, claimed that Olinger killed Jones at Pierce Canyon, not at Pope's. Owen further contended that the Pope's shooting was a separate incident involving another victim, whom he did not name.

46. Ed Bartholomew, videotaped interview with Mike Cox, Fort Davis, October 1991, in author's possession.

47. Eddins, interview. Although Eddins did not refer to the gorge by name, his description of its topography and location strongly suggests that it was Rock Corrals.

48. This study of Barney Gallagher is based on: *San Antonio Express*, 13 October 1876, copy of article in Williams Collection, Haley Library; *Austin Democratic Statesman*, 17, 18 October 1876, copies of articles in Williams Collection, Haley Library; Betsy Ross, "Historic Crossing Submerged in Dam," *Pecos Enterprise*, undated special edition, apparently a supplement to the 31 July 1936 issue; Hunter, *Trail Drivers*, 980; O'Neal, *Western Gunfighters*, 287-288; and Jay Robert Nash, *Encyclopedia of Western Lawmen and Outlaws* (New York: Paragon House, 1992), 369. "Boyd" may be John Boyd, a "professional gambler" who had been indicted in Presidio County for murder. See Sergeant L. B. Caruthers, Company E, Frontier Battalion, to Adjutant General J. B. Jones, 14 June 1880, transcripts from the office of the adjutant general of Texas, Williams Collection, Haley Library.

49. *San Antonio Express*, 19, 19 October 1876 (separate articles), and 3 November 1876, copies of articles in Williams Collection, Haley Library; and holograph (presumably by Clayton Williams) leading with "F. W. Young came to Fort Stockton . . ." in Williams Collection, Haley Library.

50. Caruthers to Jones, 14 June 1880.

51. Jno. M. Dean, county attorney, Presidio County, to O. M. Roberts, governor of Texas, 21 May 1880, transcript of letter, Williams Collection, Haley Library.

52. "Outrages and Indian Raids in Presidio County from June 1, 1879 to June 1, 1880," transcripts from the office of the adjutant general of Texas, Williams Collection, Haley Library.

53. This study of Jesse (or Jessie) Evans and the robbery of the Sender and Seibenborn store is based on "Outrages and Indian Raids," and the following transcripts from the office of the adjutant general of Texas in the Williams Collection, Haley Library: Rettlesen and Deljehan, S. and W. Schulz, Ynocente Ochoa, B. Schuster and Company, merchants, to Adjutant General Jones, 21 May 1880, telegram; Dean to Roberts, 21 May 1880; Caruthers to Nevill, 8 June 1880; Caruthers to Jones, 14 June 1880; and Lieutenant C. L. Nevill, Company E, to John B. Jones, 5 September 1880. I also drew upon Philip J. Rasch, "The Story of Jessie J. Evans," in *Panhandle-Plains Historical Review* 33 (1960), 108, 116-120.

54. This study of Clay Allison is based on: my personal inspection of the grave and tombstone, March 1993; George Coe, interview with Haley, Glencoe, New Mexico, 20 March 1927, in "Notes on the History of Southeastern New Mexico," Haley Library; Windham, interview with Haley; B. A. Oden, "Early Cowboy Days in New Mexico and Texas," typescript, Haley Library; R. D. Gage to Professor Maurice G. Fulton, 30 January 1929, original letter, Haley Library; J. L. Johnson, Sr., to Miguel A. Otero, 21 March 1929, original letter, Haley Library; W. R. Owen, interviews with Haley, 2 March 1933 and 24 June 1937; Huling Ussery, taped interview with Richard Mason, Carlsbad, New Mexico, 22 February 1982, Southwest Collection; Haley, *Rough Times*, 148-149; and Barney Hubbs, "The Day Clay Allison Died," in Chuck Parsons, *Clay Allison, Portrait of a Shootist* (Seagraves: Pioneer Book Publishers, 1983), 84-85. Location of the spring is from my interview with Haley, 4 November 1993.

55. Ussery, interview with Mason. I was unable to verify the year in which Camp took up the range land at Pope's.

56. Haley, handwritten note on the typescript of his interview with Windham; and Haley, *Rough Times*, 148.

57. Haley, taped telephone interview with author, 7 October 1992, augmented by Haley, handwritten cutline on the back of a photograph of Pope's Crossing, Haley Collection, Haley Library.

58. Eisenwine, interview. Both Pope's Camp and Pope's Crossing were on Howard Collier's property; see Conkling and Conkling, *Butterfield*, Vol. I, 379.

59. Ross, "Historic Crossing Submerged."

Chapter 3 • Emigrant Crossing

1. Mabelle Eppard Martin, "California Emigrant Roads through Texas," 287, 290-291.

2. Barney Hubbs, taped telephone interview with author, Pecos, 19 March 1992. Hubbs crossed the ford in 1908 while emigrating to a Trans-Pecos ranch with his father.

3. This study of the Emigrant Road is based on: my study of several contemporary maps, including "Map of Texas and Part of New Mexico, compiled in the Bureau of Topographical Engineers, chiefly for military purposes, 1857" (Austin: Ranger Canyon Press, n. d., facsimile reproduction), which details the routes of Marcy and Michler; "Fort Smith to Doña Aña and El Paso" (itinerary of route) in Randolph B. Marcy, *The Prairie Traveler: A Handbook for Overland Expeditions* (Williamstown: Corner House Publishers, facsimile reprint, 1968), 263-265; journal of Lieutenant Nathaniel H. Michler, *Reports of the Secretary of War with Reconnaissance of Routes from San Antonio to El Paso*, 31st Cong., 1st sess., Senate Executive Document No. 64 (Washington: 1850), 36-38 (hereinafter *Reports of the Secretary of War*); A. B. Bender, "Opening Routes Across West Texas, 1848-1850," *SHQ* 37, No. 2 (October 1933), 131-134; and Hubbs, interview with author. Information about the branch of the road from the crossing to Monument Springs (and on toward the Davis Mountains) is from correspondence between Fort Stockton

and AA general, Department of Texas, 10 December 1875, letters and telegrams sent, Fort Stockton.

4. "The Letter of Louisiana Strentzel," in Kenneth L. Holmes, ed., *Covered Wagon Women: Diaries and Letters from the Western Trails 1840-1890*, Vol. I 1840-1849 (Glendale: The Arthur H. Clark Company, 1983), 250-253; Ferol Egan, *The El Dorado Trail: The Story of the Gold Rush Routes Across Mexico* (New York: McGraw Hill Book Company, 1970), 110-114; and John Theophil Strentzel, "Biography of John Theophil Strentzel," manuscript, Haley Library. Quotes attributed to Louisiana Strentzel are from Holmes. Quotes attributed to John Theophil Strentzel are from his manuscript. Egan, citing a similar manuscript in Bancroft Library, University of California, Berkeley, dates the writing as 1890. It is unclear from the Strentzel manuscript whether all six party members died before reaching the Pecos, or before reaching California.

5. Journal of Captain Randolph B. Marcy in *Reports of the Secretary of War*, 196.

6. Journal of Michler, 38.

7. Brad C. Fowler, letter of 15 August 1853 in "Wagon Trains and Cattle Herds on the Trail in the 1850's," *WTHA Year Book* 30 (October 1954), 142. Originally published in the *Standard* (Clarksville, Texas), 1 October 1853, 2, cols. 1, 2.

8. Journal of Michler, 37-38.

9. Ibid.

10. See the maps reproduced in the Emigrant Crossing segment of the documentary film *Graveyard of the West: The Pecos River of Texas Where Myth Meets History* (Austin: Forest Glen TV Productions, Inc., 1993), written by Patrick Dearen and filmed by Glen Sample Ely.

11. George Owens, interview with Haley.

12. Fowler, letter of 15 August 1853, 144-145.

13. Captain John Pope, "Diary of the Expedition," 70.

14. Hubbs, interview with author; Hubbs, interview with Cox.

15. William Curless, "Passage of McCulloch's Emigrant Train Across the Staked Plains" (letter to the editor), *WTHA Year Book* 30 (October 1954), 150-154. Originally published in the *Dallas Herald*, 7 August 1858, 2, cols. 4, 5.

16. Ormsby, *Butterfield Overland Mail*, 68, 71.

17. Conkling and Conkling, *Butterfield*, Vol. I, 377-378.

18. Ormsby, *Butterfield Overland Mail*, 70-71.

19. Colonel George A. Armes to AA general, Department of Texas, 8 September 1879, journal of marches, scouts, and expeditions, Fort Stockton; and Armes, *Ups and Downs*, 463, 464.

20. Quotations are from my transcriptions of the original J. L. "Jeff" Glass journal, in the possession of his son, David Glass, and family, Sterling County. Background on Jeff Glass and details of the cattle drive are from my interview with David Glass, Sterling County, 13 March 1992; Melburn Glass Grigsby (with quotations from J. L. G. notebook added by Dan Glass), "The Glass Family: A Souvenir History and Genealogy 1883-1983," distributed at the Glass family Texas Centennial reunion 4 June 1983; and Melburn Glass Grigsby, compiler, and Willene Glass Boger, "The Life of James Jefferson Lafayette Glass, 1861-1947," (1967), typescript excerpt in my possession.

21. Composite of statements made by Hubbs in interviews with author and with Cox.

22. Witt, interview, 17 July 1993. Rocky Crossing, situated three to four miles below the present U.S. Highway 80 bridge, provided passage to Cross C cowboys bound for roundups at west-side ranches such as the Elmer Jones spread. "It was a well-known crossing in my day," noted Witt. "It was in what we called the Upper River Pasture where we used to keep our saddle horses. It was about knee-deep to

a horse and almost solid gravel in the bottom. You could cross there in a wagon. Then you had to go all the way to Emigrant Crossing to cross it without swimming a horse."

23. Pope, "Diary of the Expedition," 70.

24. *50th Anniversary West of the Pecos Rodeo, 50-Year History Edition* (1979) (otherwise unidentified clipping in my possession), 90.

25. U.S. Geological Survey, Ligon Ranch Quadrangle, 7.5-minute series (topographic map).

26. This account of the discovery of the skull is based on: Barney Hubbs, interview with author; Hubbs, interview with Cox; and Hubbs, "Indian Burial Grounds, Immigrant Crossing on the Pecos, Rancher Discovers Skeletons," cutlines on a photo display at West of the Pecos Museum, Pecos. Although the cutlines are uncredited, they are written on paper bearing the letterhead of Barney Hubbs.

27. Hubbs, interview with author. In his cursory examination of the skeletons, Hubbs found no evidence of mutilation. The quote regarding exhumation by coyotes is from Hubbs, interview with Cox.

28. Hubbs, interview with author.

29. Ibid.

30. See *Graveyard of the West*, Howard's Well segment.

31. Composite of statements by Hubbs in interviews with author and with Cox.

32. Clayton Williams, *Last Frontier*, 231.

33. Ibid., 164, citing Jno. P. Hatch, Fort Concho, to AA general, Department of Texas, 2 August 1872, Army Commands, RG 98, National Archives.

34. L. E. Edwards (for J. A. McMillan) to the commandant of post of Fort Stockton, 22 March 1873, letters and telegrams received, Fort

Stockton.

35. Post returns, April 1873, Fort Stockton.

36. Ibid.; and post returns, March 1873, Fort Stockton.

37. Captain Charles A. Wikoff to post adjutant, 8 July 1873, letters and telegrams received, Fort Stockton.

38. Headquarters, Department of Texas, to Fort Stockton headquarters, 28 July 1873, letters and telegrams received, Fort Stockton.

39. Hubbs, "Indian Burial Grounds."

40. See Dearen, *Castle Gap*, 111-129.

41. My inspection of site, November 1991.

42. Ibid.

43. Hubbs, interview with Cox.

Cahpter 4 • Horsehead Crossing

1. Charles Goodnight, as quoted in Haley, *Goodnight*, 134; and Hubbs, interview with Cox. For a companion discussion of Horsehead Crossing, see Dearen, *Castle Gap*, 35-61.

2. Dobie, *Vaquero*, 274.

3. Stephen Powers, Afoot and Alone: *A Walk from Sea to Sea by the Southern Route* (Hartford, Conn.: Columbian Book Company, 1886), 142.

4. Mabelle Eppard Martin, ed., "From Texas to California in 1849: Diary of C. C. Cox," *SHQ* 29 (July 1925), 45-46.

5. Powers, *Afoot and Alone*, 142.

6. Ruth Shackleford diary as contained in Kenneth L. Holmes, ed., *Covered Wagon Women*, Vol. 9 1864-1868, 192.

7. For a discussion on Castle Gap, see Dearen, *Castle Gap*, 3-34.

8. O. W. Williams, *Pioneer Surveyor*, 278; Haley, *Fort Concho and the Texas Frontier* (San Angelo: San Angelo Standard-Times, 1952), 2-3, 5, 7.

9. Albert D. Richardson, *Beyond the Mississippi* (Hartford: American Publishing Company, 1867), 233.

10. John Salmon Ford, *Rip Ford's Texas* (Austin: University of Texas Press, 1963), 123. For a discussion of other possible origins of the skulls, see Dearen, *Castle Gap*, 39.

11. James W. Mullens, interview with Haley, 14 January 1927, Roswell, New Mexico, typescript, Haley Library.

12. Martin, "California Emigrant Roads Through Texas," 294.

13. Martin, ed., "Diary of C. C. Cox," 36-38.

14. Ibid., 45-46.

15. Mabelle Eppard Martin, ed., "From Texas to California in 1849: Lewis B. Harris to a Brother," *SHQ* 29, No. 3 (January 1926), 216.

16. Martin, ed., "Diary of C. C. Cox," 46-47.

17. Martin, ed., "Lewis B. Harris to a Brother," 216.

18. George Owens, interview with Haley.

19. Rachel Eads, "A Trying Trip Across the Desert," *Frontier Times* 22, No. 9 (June 1945), 243-244.

20. "Diary of Oscar Call, July 8-August 4, 1858," *Stalking Kin* 2, No. 4, 167-168, West Texas Collection, Angelo State University, San Angelo, Texas.

21. Charles Kenner, "The Origins of the 'Goodnight' Trail Reconsidered," *SHQ* 77, No. 3 (January 1974), 390-394. By 1866, an estimated 3,111,475 beeves grazed Texas ranges and could be purchased for $3 to $5 a head, while northern markets offered the promise of much higher prices. See *The Texas Almanac for 1867* (Galveston: The Galveston News), 197.

22. Irbin H. Bell, interview with Haley, 18 March 1927, El Paso, in "Notes Upon the Cross Timber Country," Haley Library.

23. Oliver Loving to R. M. Garden, Weatherford, 22 May 1866, original letter, Haley Library. The last name of the recipient is in question, due to variant interpretations of Loving's script.

24. Date of reoccupation is as stated in post returns, Fort Stockton, July 1867, microfilm, Southwest Collection. A variant date of 21 July 1867 turns up in Brevet Major General Edward Hatch's letter to Charles E. Morse, AAA general, 20 February 1868, letters and telegrams sent, Fort Stockton.

25. Edward Hatch to AAA general, District of Texas, 5 August 1867, letters sent, headquarters records, Fort Stockton.

26. Captain George Gamble to post adjutant, 20 August 1867, letters received, Fort Stockton.

27. First Lieutenant Fred W. Smith, Ninth U.S. Cavalry, report of scout, 22 October 1867, letters received, Fort Stockton.

28. Fort Stockton headquarters to Brevet Lieutenant Colonel William S. Abert, AA general, District of Texas, 31 August 1867, letters sent, Fort Stockton.

29. Shackleford diary, 187-189.

30. Powers, *Afoot and Alone*, xvi, 19, 136, 140-143. I gained important background on Powers's journey from Harwood Hinton, telephone interview, Austin, summer 1993.

31. Shackleford diary, 190-191.

32. Ibid., 191.

33. San Antonio *Herald*, 18 April 1868, as cited by Clayton Williams, *Last Frontier*, 91.

34. Shackleford diary, 191-193.

35. Ibid., 193.

36. Cora Addison Posey, "Another Trail Driver: William Hinton Posey," *Frontier Times* 8, No. 5 (February 1931), 216-217.

37. Hunter, *Trail Drivers*, 1029.

38. D. N. Arnett, interview with Haley, Colorado City, 18 October 1926, in "South Plains Interviews," Haley Library.

39. Ibid.

40. C. J. White, interview with Haley, Sheridan, Wyoming, 22 April 1928, in "Notes Upon the Cross Timber Country," Haley Library.

41. W. C. Cochran, "A Long Cattle Drive to Montana," *Frontier Times* 22, No. 9 (June 1945), 253-255.

42. Bell, interview with Haley.

43. Shrode journal in *Ho for California!*, 269-270.

44. Cross, "Breaking a Stampede," 275.

45. Columbus Fleming Barton, record written for the Barton family reunion, San Saba County, 1941, as contained in "The Columbus Fleming Barton Family," a section of an unidentified clipping in my possession.

46. G. W. Roberson, interview with Haley, 30 June 1926, Vega, in "Panhandle Notes, Volume 2," Haley Library.

47. Captain F. S. Dodge to AAA general, 13 May 1873, letters and telegrams sent, Fort Stockton. Drovers who did gain escort invariably made it through with their herds. In November 1873, for example, drovers guarded by a Fort Stockton lieutenant and fifteen men successfully pushed up the Pecos. See outgoing correspondence from Fort Stockton headquarters, 13 November 1873, letters and telegrams sent, Fort Stockton.

48. Post returns, Fort Stockton, August 1874, Southwest Collection.

49. "Journal of scout of detachment, Company M, 9th Cavalry, commanded by Second Lieutenant Thomas Davenport, 9th Cavalry, from Fort Stockton, Texas to Pecos Falls, via Horsehead Crossing, returning via Frazier Crossing and Monument Springs, pursuant to special order . . . dated March 16, 1874," journal of marches, scouts, and expeditions, Fort Stockton.

50. *San Antonio Express*, 23 December 1877, copy of article in Williams Collection, Haley Library.

51. Ibid.; Lieutenant Colonel M. M. Blunt to AA general, Department of Texas, 21 December 1877, letters and telegrams sent, Fort Stockton.

52. Second Lieutenant C. Esterly, Tenth Cavalry, to post adjutant, Fort Stockton, 16 October 1878, journals of marches, scouts, and expeditions, Fort Stockton.

53. Armes, *Ups and Downs*, 463, 466.

54. Second Lieutenant John Bigelow to adjutant general, 9 December 1879, journal of marches, scouts, and expeditions, Fort Stockton.

55. Hunter, *Trail Drivers*, 466.

56. W. F. Kellis, "Our Criminal Record Since Early Days," *Sterling City News-Record*, 24 April 1936; and W. F. Kellis, "Chronicles of Early Days," *Sterling City News-Record*, 11 December 1942.

57. Kellis, "Our Criminal Record." The date of Kellis's arrival in the North Concho valley is from Kellis, *Sterling City News-Record*, 17 December 1943.

58. Hunter, *Trail Drivers*, 678-679.

59. Erving McElroy, taped interview with David Murrah, Lubbock, 1 June 1972, Southwest Collection. Although McElroy does not name the ford where the incident occurred, Horsehead was the only crossing along a direct line between the McElroy Ranch and Fort Stockton.

60. Russell Dyer, taped interview with Paul Patterson, Sanderson, summer 1968, Southwest Collection.

61. Tyson Midkiff, composite of statements made in taped interview with author, Rankin, 9 August 1989; taped telephone interview with author, Rankin, 11 December 1990; and videotaped interview with author, Rankin, 29 April 1991.

62. Walter Boren, taped interview with author, Post, 8 August 1990.

63. Gid Reding, taped interview with author, Fort Stockton, 1 September 1989. Although the article "Legendary Pecos crossing located," *Austin American-Statesman*, 20 March 1995 (Associated Press, originating at the *Odessa American*) implies that Horsehead Crossing and the stage stand site had recently been rediscovered by Bill Boyd of Crane, the locations pinpointed by Boyd were already well known. See Patrick Dearen, "Horsehead to Castle Gap: Trailing the Past," *True West* 39, 8 (August 1992), 22-27. Based in part on Dearen's search by canoe with Richard Galle in early spring 1990, and on Dearen's extensive ground search with Galle and Rick Gray on 2 June 1991 (and numerous earlier solo searches by Dearen), the *True West* article notes the location of the 1869 crossing and the location of the stage stand. For a visual look at the 1869 crossing's location, see the Horsehead Crossing segment (filmed 19 October 1991 and 18 November 1991) of *Graveyard of the West*. For a much earlier pinpointing of the stage stand site, see Clayton Williams, "That Topographical Ghost—Horsehead Crossing!," *The Permian Historical Annual*, Vol. 17 (December 1977), 37-56, especially the

October 2, 1973 map by J. E. Beck on page 44. Boyd's metal detector finds (beginning in August 1993) and later archaeological finds by Joe Allen of Crane confirm pioneer presence at the respective sites pinpointed by Williams, Dearen, and Ely. Those artifacts are on display at Crane County Historical Museum in Crane.

64. Chon Villalba, taped interview with author, Fort Stockton, 9 February 1990.

65. Clayton Williams, *Last Frontier*, 164. Also, Bliss to AA general, 19 November 1872, Army Commands, RG 98, National Archives.

66. Villalba, interview.

67. However, in 1948 or 1949, well into the mechanized era of ranching, Leslie McFadden, Sam Tanner, and another cowboy crossed less than one hundred cows from east to west at a site they presumed to be Horsehead in a fifteen-mile, one-day drive that ended at Tanner's spread several miles above the ford. McFadden found a 250-yard straightaway suitable for crossing the gravel-bottomed river, which at the time was too shallow to swim his horse. McFadden described the east side as gently sloping and the west as without an appreciable bank. He pinpointed the site as approximately one-half mile upstream of the present historical marker. (Leslie McFadden, interview with author, Rankin, 21 August 1995.)

Chapter 5 • Spanish Dam Crossing

1. This description of the Great Rock and its immediate surroundings is based on my investigation of the site, 19 October 1991; my study of topographic maps, including U.S. Geological Survey, McCamey South Quadrangle, 7.5-minute series; Juan Dominguez de Mendoza's journal in Bolton, *Spanish Exploration*, 331; and O. W. Williams, *Mendosa*, 18-19.

2. Newland, interview with Kelton.

3. O. W. Williams, *Mendosa*, 4, 22.

4. Bolton, *Spanish Exploration*, 329-330.

5. J. W. Williams, *Old Texas Trails*, 191; O. W. Williams, *Mendosa*, 17-18; and Victor J. Smith, "Early Spanish Exploration, 63. The height of the hill is from U. S. Geological Survey, McCamey South Quadrangle (topographic map).

6. Bolton, *Spanish Exploration*, 330-332.

7. Based on my study of the topography of Spanish Dam's immediate vicinity, as indicated by U.S. Geological Survey, McCamey South Quadrangle (topographic map).

8. Bolton, *Spanish Exploration*, 331-332.

9. Ibid., 332.

10. H. C. K., *San Antonio Daily Express*, 25 May 1877, in Williams Collection, Haley Library.

11. Clayton Williams, "The First Two Irrigation Projects on the Pecos River in Texas," *The Permian Historical Annual* 15 (December 1975), 4. Also see *Lands of Texas*, Vol. 8, Chapter 43, 449 (as approved by the Texas State Legislature 10 March 1875).

12. Clayton Williams, *Last Frontier*, 205, 207.

13. Ibid., 195; and Clayton Williams, "The First Two Irrigation Projects," 2.

14. *San Antonio Daily Express*, 25 May 1877.

15. Ibid.; and my personal investigation of site. Information about the frame of possible cypress is from Randy Summerlin, "Pecos River Dam One of Earliest," *San Angelo Standard-Times*, undated clipping in my possession.

16. *San Antonio Daily Express*, 25 May 1877; and U.S. Geological Survey, McCamey South Quadrangle (topographic map). A 1941 inspection by W. R. Baggett, Monroe Baggett, and Curtis Van Zandt found the ditch about twelve feet wide and five feet deep where it

left the river: W. R. Baggett, "Early Day Irrigation Ditches on the Pecos," *Frontier Times* 19, No. 10 (July 1942), 364. In my own inspection, I judged the canal approximately fifteen feet wide just below the dam.

17. Billy Rankin, videotaped interview with author, Rankin, 29 April 1991.

18. Newland, interview with Kelton.

19. *San Antonio Daily Express*, 25 May 1877; and Baggett, "Early Day Irrigation Ditches," 365. The size of the Torres labor force is from Clayton Williams, "The Pontoon Bridge on the Pecos, 1869-1886," *The Permian Historical Annual* 18 (December 1978), 15, citing *The Fort Stockton Pioneer*, 10 September 1908 and 17 September 1908.

20. Lieutenant W. H. Beck to post adjutant, Fort Stockton, 11 August 1878, journal of marches, scouts, and expeditions, Fort Stockton.

21. Baggett, "Early Day Irrigation Ditches," 364-366.

22. Ibid., 365. By the fall of 1880, the farming project covered 1,000 acres, and its eighteen miles of lateral ditches had the capacity to irrigate 2,000 acres more. See "Pecos County 28 Years Ago," *The Fort Stockton Pioneer*, 10 September and 17 September 1908 (reprint of article in *Texas Sun* of San Antonio, November-December 1880), microfilm, Library, University of Texas of the Permian Basin, Odessa.

23. *San Antonio Express*, 4 May 1877, as cited in Clayton Williams, *Last Frontier*, 210-211.

24. H. C. K., *San Antonio Daily Express*, 18 May 1877, in Williams Collection, Haley Library.

25. *San Antonio Express*, 14 August 1877, in Williams Collection, Haley Library. Also see Clayton Williams, *Last Frontier*, 213, citing *San Antonio Express*, 17, 22, and 30 August 1877.

26. Baggett, "Early Day Irrigation Ditches," 364-365.

27. *San Angelo Standard*, 13 September 1884, 4, col. 3.

28. Baggett, "Early Day Irrigation Ditches," 366. Baggett gained his information from Arthur Young.

29. Nora Locklin, taped telephone interview with author, McCamey, 26 March 1992. Mrs. Locklin recalled that when she moved to a ranch a short distance downstream in 1931 the outline of the dam was still "fairly plain."

30. "The Last Spike Driven and the Southern Pacific Route is Complete," *San Antonio Daily Express*, 13 January 1883.

31. O. W. Williams, *Mendosa*, 18. Cora Dawson Smith, familiar with Horsehead Crossing a half-mile above her family ranch of the early 1900s, concurred that Spanish Dam "was easier to get across" and thus favored by travelers of that time. Cora Dawson Smith, taped interview with author, Iraan, 12 August 1982.

32. Midkiff, interview, 29 April 1991.

33. Rankin, interview, 29 April 1991.

34. Newland, interview with Kelton.

35. Ibid.

36. O. W. Williams, *Mendosa*, 18-19.

37. Baggett, "Early Day Irrigation Ditches," 366; William B. Wilson, taped telephone interview with author, Midland, 28 November 1994; and U. S. Geological Survey, 7.5-minute series, Indian Mesa Quadrangle (topographic map).

38. Roy McDonald, taped interview with author, Pecos County, 12 August 1982.

39. Wilson, interview.

40. Billy Rankin, taped telephone interview with author, Rankin, 28

November 1994.

Chapter 6 • Pontoon Crossing

1. Second Lieutenant Ira W. Trask, assistant post adjutant, to Captain F. S. Dodge, 3 May 1868, letters and telegrams sent, Fort Stockton.

2. Report of Captain F. S. Dodge, Ninth Cavalry, 15 May 1868, letters and telegrams received, Fort Stockton.

3. Brevet Major General Edward Hatch to Captain George Gamble, 1 July 1868, letters and telegrams received, Fort Stockton.

4. Report of F. S. Dodge, 24 July 1868, letters and telegrams received, Fort Stockton.

5. Site of crossing is from Brevet Lieutenant Colonel Thomas B. Hunt, "Journal showing the Route taken by the Government Train accompanying the 15th Regiment U.S. Infantry From Austin, Texas to Fort Craig, New Mexico and returning to San Antonio, July-December 1869," 28 (entries and sketch map), Q-154, Record Group 77, National Archives, Washington, D. C.; and U. S. Geological Survey, Table Top Mountain Quadrangle, 7.5-minute series (topographic map).

6. Ira W. Trask, post adjutant, to Lieutenant Robert Neely, 31 August 1868, letters and telegrams sent, Fort Stockton.

7. H. C. Logan, *San Antonio Herald*, 10 November 1868, as quoted in Clayton Williams, *Last Frontier*, 104; and Clayton Williams, "The Pontoon Bridge," 6.

8. Major James Wade, Ninth Cavalry, to Captain C. E. Morse, AAA General, 16 June 1869, letters and telegrams sent, Fort Stockton. Distance is based on my study of U. S. Geological Survey, Table Top Mountain Quadrangle (topographic map), and the journal of Thomas B. Hunt, 28 (sketch map).

9. Journal of Thomas B. Hunt, 28.

10. Measurements are from Clayton Williams, "The Pontoon Bridge," 9 (sketch map); and Grover C. Ramsey, "Camp Melvin, Crockett County, Texas," *WTHA Year Book* 37 (October 1961), 141, 146. Ramsey cites headquarters, Fifth Military District, Austin, General Order No. 66, 31 March 1869.

11. Paul Patterson, taped interview with author, Pecos, 1 July 1993.

12. Tom Vandevanter, taped telephone interview with author, Rankin, 19 March 1993.

13. Extracts from a letter of Major C. M. Tunnel, paymaster, Fort Concho, 21 October 1869, in E. D. Judd, paymaster's office, Fifth Military District, to Brevet Colonel H. Clay Wood, AA general, 11 November 1869, letters and telegrams received, Fort Stockton. Distance from Lancaster Bridge to Melvin is from the journal of Thomas B. Hunt, 28-29.

14. Captain George Gamble to Brevet Captain C. S. Roberts, AAA general, 8 December 1868, letters and telegrams sent, Fort Stockton.

15. Harriet Bunyard diary in Holmes, ed., *Covered Wagon Women*, Vol. 9, 211, 228 (Holmes erroneously gives the date of Harriet's journey as 1868).

16. Harriet Bunyard diary in Myres, ed., *Ho for California!*, 214; Wade to Morse, 16 June 1869.

17. Bunyard diary in Myres, *Ho for California!*, 214.

18. Wrote Tunnel: "I measured the river carefully at Melvin and found it as follows: waterline (surface of water) at the crossing where tramping of animals has somewhat increased the width, 48 feet 6 inches. From top of bank to top of bank 30 feet above ferry, 53.6. From top of bank to top of bank 30 feet below ferry, 40.6." See extracts from a letter of Major C. M. Tunnel, 21 October 1869.

19. Ibid.

20. Wrote Grover: "I think the road can be shortened about 10 miles and otherwise improved by crossing the Pecos from 5 to 6 miles above the old mail station [Pecos Mail Station], near where the road from Stockton first strikes the river. There is a gap through the bluffs on the left bank." Brevet Major General C. Grover to Fort Stockton headquarters, 23 January 1870, letters and telegrams received, Fort Stockton.

21. Ibid. Humfreville already was drawing up plans and a detailed estimate.

22. Fort Davis surgeon's report, 2 June 1870, as quoted in Clayton Williams, "The Pontoon Bridge," 12.

23. Shelby, commanding Grierson Springs, to Fort Concho headquarters, 16 January 1882, copy of telegram in Colonel Benjamin Grierson to commanding officer, Fort Stockton, 16 January 1882, letters and telegrams received, Fort Stockton.

24. O. W. Williams, *Pioneer Surveyor*, 101.

25. "Journal of march of detachment, Company M, 9th Cavalry, commanded by Second Lieutenant Thomas C. Davenport, 9th U.S. Cavalry, from Fort Stockton, Texas to Independence Creek viz. old Fort Lancaster . . . pursuant to special order number 14, headquarters, Fort Stockton, Texas, February 4, 1874," journal of marches, scouts, and expeditions, Fort Stockton.

26. August Santleben, *A Texas Pioneer* (New York: Neal Publishing Company, 1910), 145. Santleben erroneously identifies the site as Horsehead Crossing.

27. Fort Davis surgeon's report, 2 June 1870.

28. Sandra L. Myres, ed., "A Woman's View of the Texas Frontier, 1874: The Diary of Emily K. Andrews," *SHQ* 86, No. 1 (July 1982), 49-50, 72.

29. My inspection of site, 19 November 1991.

30. C. Babcock, "San Antonio and El Paso Mail Line and its

Connections," *The Texas Almanac* for 1870 (Galveston: Galveston News), 141.

31. Journal of Thomas B. Hunt, 28. Hunt referred to it as "Camp Melbourne."

32. Post returns, May 1871, Fort Stockton, Southwest Collection.

33. Post returns, January 1872, Fort Stockton, Southwest Collection.

34. Post returns, January 1876 through October 1879, Fort Stockton, Southwest Collection.

35. Captain F. S. Dodge to AA general's office, Department of Texas, 1 September 1873, letters and telegrams sent, Fort Stockton.

36. Clayton Williams, "The Pontoon Bridge," 14, citing Joseph Carrol McConnell, *The West Texas Frontier*, Vol. II (Jacksboro: 1933-1939), 309-310.

37. Captain E. G. Bush to AA general, 2 July 1874, letters and telegrams sent, Fort Stockton.

38. E. G. Bush to AAA general, Department of Texas, 2 July 1874, letters and telegrams sent, Fort Stockton.

39. Babcock, *The Texas Almanac* for 1870, 141.

40. James B. Gillett, *Six Years with the Texas Rangers, 1875 to 1881* (New Haven: Yale University Press, 1925), 148.

41. "The Indian Raiders, The Missing Stage Not Yet Found—More 'Sign,'" *San Antonio Daily Express*, 28 October 1877, microfilm, Library, Angelo State University, San Angelo.

42. Lieutenant Colonel M. M. Blunt to AA general, 29 October 1877, letters and telegrams sent, Fort Stockton; M. M. Blunt to AA general, 2 November 1877, letters and telegrams sent, Fort Stockton; and "The Missing El Paso Stage Coach Found, The Driver Murdered, the Horses Stolen and Registered Packages Gone Through With,"

San Antonio Daily Express, 31 October 1877, Angelo State University, San Angelo. The name of the slain driver is from "Record of Engagement with Hostile Indians in Texas, 1868-1882," *WTHA Year Book* 9 (October 1933), 114. Although the latter gives the date of the slaying as 1878, other details point to a common incident.

43. Captain D. D. Van Valzah to AAA general, District of Pecos, Fort Concho, 28 June 1878, letters and telegrams sent, Fort Stockton. Van Valzah reported the wounded cowhand in critical condition at Fort Stockton.

44. Van Valzah to AA general, 28 June 1878, letters and telegrams sent, Fort Stockton; Lieutenant W. H. Beck to post adjutant, 11 August 1878, journal of marches, scouts, and expeditions, Fort Stockton; and Clayton Williams, "The Pontoon Bridge," 15, citing *Galveston Daily News*, 28 June 1878.

45. Van Valzah to AAA general, 28 June 1878.

46. Beck to post adjutant, 11 August 1878.

47. Taylor to commanding officer, Fort Stockton, 2 January 1877, letters and telegrams received, Fort Stockton.

48. Van Valzah to AA general, 2 January 1877, and to AA general, 3 January 1877, letters and telegrams sent, Fort Stockton.

49. Post returns, November 1877, Fort Stockton, Southwest Collection.

50. M. M. Blunt to AA general, 28 December 1877, letters and telegrams sent, Fort Stockton.

51. Post returns, February 1878 and March 1878, Fort Stockton, Southwest Collection.

52. Van Valzah to AAA general, 28 June 1878, letters and telegrams sent, Fort Stockton.

53. Post returns, July 1878, Fort Stockton, Southwest Collection.

54. Lieutenant Maxon to commanding officer, Fort Concho, 15 August 1880, copy in Haley Collection, Haley Library.

55. R. F. O'Beirne to AA general, 11 and 13 September 1880, letters and telegrams sent, Fort Stockton.

56. Ripley, post adjutant, to Major E. D. Baker, quartermaster, San Antonio, 28 September 1880, letters and telegrams sent, Fort Stockton.

57. Post returns, January and March 1880, Fort Stockton.

58. Shelby, commanding Grierson Springs, to post adjutant, Fort Concho, 16 January 1882, (copy of telegram in Grierson to commanding officer, Fort Stockton, 16 January 1882).

59. Captain S. T. Norvell to AA general, 15 October 1875, letters and telegrams sent, Fort Stockton.

60. Grierson to commanding officer, Fort Stockton, 16 January 1882, with copy of Shelby to post adjutant, Fort Concho, 16 January 1882.

61. George Owens, interview with Haley.

62. *San Angelo Standard*, 21 February 1885, 2, col. 2.

63. Locklin, interview, 26 March 1992.

64. Newland, interview with Kelton. Newland worked for James Currie.

65. Mrs. Will (Opal) Nix, taped interview with Paul Patterson, Rankin, 30 May 1968, Southwest Collection.

66. Ed Bartholomew, videotaped interview with Mike Cox, Fort Davis, October 1991, copy in my possession. Considering the improbability that the long-neglected bridge could have supported automobiles by that time, Bartholomew observed that Draper "might have even built another bridge there after a fashion."

67. Bill Drake, surveyor, report to the commissioner of the General Land Office of Texas, 19 November 1911, quoted in a sketch map in Clayton Williams, "The Pontoon Bridge," 9.

68. Ramsey, "Camp Melvin," 146.

69. Bartholomew, interview with Cox.

70. Vandevanter, interview.

71. My inspection of site.

72. Ramsey, "Camp Melvin," 145.

73. Vandevanter, interview.

74. "A Daring Hold Up," *El Paso Daily Times*, 15 May 1897, Library, University of Texas of the Permian Basin, Odessa.

75. Vandevanter, interview.

76. William Edward Syers, *Off the Beaten Trail* (Waco: Texian Press, 1971), 404-406.

77. The map is reproduced in *Western Chronicles* 3, No. 1 (Pecos County Historical Commission, fall 1981), 2.

78. *1990-91 Texas Almanac* (Dallas: The Dallas Morning News, 1989), 60.

Chapter 7 • Lancaster Crossing

1. Journal of William H. C. Whiting in Ralph P. Bieber, ed., *Exploring Southwestern Trails 1846-1854* (Glendale: Arthur H. Clark Company, 1938), 258-261; Report of Brevet Second Lieutenant William F. Smith in *Reports of the Secretary of War*, 4-5. I also drew upon U.S.G.S. topographic maps and my investigation of the site, 2 August 1993. The ford is situated approximately one-half mile below the present U.S. Highway 290 bridge and near the intersection of

Pecos, Terrell, and Crockett counties.

2. Fort Stockton commander to AA general, Department of Texas, 11 September 1880, letters and telegrams sent, Fort Stockton. The crossing is referred to as "the Lancaster ford" in Major R. F. O'Beirne to AA general, Department of Texas, 11 September 1880, letters and telegrams sent, Fort Stockton.

3. Second Lieutenant John P. Sherburne, Fort Lancaster, to Major D. H. Vinton, chief quartermaster of Texas, 27 May 1857, RG 94, National Archives; and "Overland Mail Route Between San Antonio, Texas, and San Diego, California," *The Texas Almanac* for 1859 (Galveston: The Galveston News), 146.

4. Journal of William H. C. Whiting, 262, 337-338.

5. Report of William F. Smith, 7.

6. Haley, ed., *The Diary of Michael Erskine* (Haley Library, 1979), 160 ("Memo of Mr. Campbell's Route to California"); and James G. Bell diary in Haley, ed., "A Log of the Texas-California Cattle Trail, 1854," *SHQ* 35, No. 3 (January 1932), 219. More specifically, Campbell refers to it as "the crossing of the Pacus," and Bell terms it "the crossing of the Pecos Rio."

7. Journal of Captain Edward S. Meyer in Escal F. Duke, ed., "A Description of the Route from San Antonio to El Paso by Captain Edward S. Meyer," *WTHA Year Book* 49 (1973), 129, 136.

8. Lieutenant Colonel J. E. Johnston's report, including "List of encamping places on the southern route from San Antonio to El Paso, with distances," *Reports of the Secretary of War*, 29.

9. Olin Smith, taped telephone interview with author, Sheffield, December 1992, and taped interview with author, Terrell and Pecos counties, 2 August 1993.

10. Report of William F. Smith, 5.

11. Journal of William H. C. Whiting, 260.

12. Ibid., 261.

13. Ibid., 264-265. The distance is from *The Texas Almanac* for 1859, 146; and journal of Captain Edward S. Meyer, 129.

14. Report of Captain S. G. French, *Reports of the Secretary of War*, 45-46, 53.

15. Ibid., 52; and report of J. E. Johnston, 27.

16. Journal of Captain Edward S. Meyer, 129.

17. Report of J. E. Johnston, 27.

18. "The Report of Edward Fitzgerald Beale to the Secretary of War Concerning the Wagon Road from Fort Defiance to the Colorado River" in Lewis Burt Lesley, ed., *Uncle Sam's Camels: The Journal of May Humphreys Stacey* (Cambridge: Harvard University Press, 1929), 154-155.

19. J. Frank Bowles, "Overland Trip to California in 1850," *Frontier Times* 4, No. 5 (February 1927), 12.

20. Jack C. Scannell, "Henry Skillman, Texas Frontiersman," *The Permian Historical Annual* 18 (December 1978), 21-23.

21. Frank Bishop Lammons, "Operation Camel: An Experiment in Animal Transportation in Texas, 1857-1860," SHQ 61, No. 1 (July 1957), 22.

22. Sherburne to Vinton, 27 May 1857.

23. Colonel Joseph K. F. Mansfield's report in Robert W. Frazer, ed., *Mansfield on the Condition of the Western Forts 1853-54* (Norman: University of Oklahoma Press, 1963), 29.

24. *The Colorado Tribune* (Matagorda), 21 July 1854, copy of article, Haley Collection, Haley Library.

25. Haley, ed., *The Diary of Michael Erskine*, 160 ("Memo of Mr. Campbell's Route").

26. *The Colorado Tribune*, 21 July 1854.

27. *The Galveston Journal*, 26 May 1854, copy of article in Haley Collection, Haley Library.

28. *The Colorado Tribune*, 21 July 1854.

29. Haley, ed., *The Diary of Michael Erskine*, 31, 34 (introduction by Haley), and 49, 69 (diary entries).

30. James G. Bell diary, 210, 219, 221.

31. Department of Texas Special Order No. 79, 20 July 1855, RG 94, National Archives; post returns, August 1855, Fort Lancaster, National Archives, microfilm in my possession. At least two later records give the date of occupation as 21 August 1855. See Sherburne to Vinton, 27 May 1857; and "Colonel J. K. F. Mansfield's Report of the Inspection of the Department of Texas," *SHQ* 42, No. 3 (January 1939), 255.

32. Sherburne to Vinton, 27 May 1857.

33. Barry Scobee, *Old Fort Davis* (San Antonio: Naylor Company, 1947), 11.

34. Post returns, December 1855, Fort Lancaster, National Archives, microfilm in my possession.

35. "Colonel J. K. F. Mansfield's Report of the Inspection of the Department of Texas in 1856," *SHQ* 42, No. 2 (October 1938), 131; and "Colonel J. K. F. Mansfield's Report of the Inspection of the Department of Texas in 1856," *SHQ* 42, No. 3 (January 1939), 251, 253.

36. Ibid., 255-256.

37. Department of Texas Order No. 53, 21 August 1856, RG 94, National Archives. Also see post returns, September 1856, Fort Lancaster, National Archives, microfilm in my possession.

38. John C. Reid, *Reid's Tramp, or a Journal of the Incidents of Ten Months Travel Through Texas, New Mexico, Arizona, Sonora, and California* (Austin: Steck Company, 1935), 115-116.

39. Ibid., 114-116.

40. Report of Edward Fitzgerald Beale, *Uncle Sam's Camels*, 157-158.

41. Journal of May Humphreys Stacey, *Uncle Sam's Camels*, 59.

42. Report of Edward Fitzgerald Beale, *Uncle Sam's Camels*, 158-160.

43. Zenas R. Bliss, "Reminiscences" Vol. 2, 21, 22-23, (five volumes) Williams Collection, Haley Library.

44. "Overland Mail Route," *The Texas Almanac* for 1859, 139-150. Information about Skillman yielding the original line to Giddings is from Wayne R. Austerman, "Giddings' Station, A Forgotten Landmark on the Pecos," *The Permian Historical Annual* 21 (1981), 5.

45. Emmie Giddings W. Mahon and Chester V. Kielman, "Giddings and the San Antonio-San Diego Mail Line," SHQ 61, No. 2 (October 1957), 231-232.

46. "Overland Mail Route," *The Texas Almanac* for 1859, 139, 149.

47. San Antonio and San Diego Mail advertisement reproduced in Clayton Williams, *Never Again* Vol. 3 (San Antonio: Naylor Company, 1969).

48. Post returns, June and November 1858, and January 1859, Fort Lancaster, National Archives, microfilm in my possession; journal of Captain Edward S. Meyer, 129.

49. Clayton Williams, *Last Frontier*, 64. The distance from Escondido Springs to Fort Stockton is from the journal of Captain Edward S. Meyer, 129.

50. Brevet Major General Edward Hatch to Lieutenant C. E. Morse,

AAA general, District of Texas, 18 November 1867, letters and telegrams sent, Fort Stockton.

51. Inspector General Joseph K. F. Mansfield, inspection report of Fort Lancaster, Texas, 21 November 1860, RG 94, National Archives.

52. Post returns, January 1861, Fort Lancaster, National Archives, microfilm in my possession.

53. Special Order No. 32 from headquarters, Department of Texas, San Antonio, Texas, 24 February 1861, in *The War of the Rebellion*, series 1, 1:594. The date of the vote for secession is from Crawford, "A History of West Texas," 43.

54. Post returns, March 1861, Fort Lancaster, National Archives, microfilm in my possession.

55. W. W. Heartsill, *Fourteen Hundred and 91 Days in the Confederate Army: A Journal Kept by W. W. Heartsill for Four Years, One Month and One Day* (Jackson: McCowat-Mercer Press, facsimile edition of original 1876 edition, 1953), 48-51.

56. Ibid, 50-51.

57. *A History of Crockett County* (San Angelo: Crockett County Historical Society American Revolution Bicentennial Project, Anchor Publishing Company, 1976), 28.

58. J. Marvin Hunter, "Midnight Battle at Fort Lancaster," *Frontier Times* 21, No. 9 (June 1944), 367 (a letter, evidently published in its entirety, from H. W. Halleck, Headquarters of the Army, Washington, D.C., to Brigadier General Carlton, Santa Fe, New Mexico).

59. Ibid., 368-370; and R. H. Williams, *With the Border Ruffians: Memories of the Far West, 1852-1868*, E. W. Williams, ed., (London: John Murray, 1908), 363-372. The two accounts vary slightly in certain details. R. H. Williams was a member of the victorious Texas party.

60. Journal of Edward S. Meyer, 128, 136.

61. Distance is from journal of Captain Edward S. Meyer, 129. Date of reoccupation is from post returns, July 1867, Fort Stockton, Southwest Collection.

62. Hatch to Lieutenant C. E. Morse, AAA general, District of Texas, 18 November 1867, letters and telegrams sent, Fort Stockton.

63. Hatch to Brevet Colonel James F. Wade, 8 December 1867, letters and telegrams sent, Fort Stockton.

64. Hatch to Morse, AAA general, District of Texas, 14 December 1867, letters and telegrams sent, Fort Stockton.

65. Fort Stockton headquarters correspondence of 23 January 1870, referred to Brevet Major General C. Grover, AAA general, Fifth Military District, letters and telegrams received, Fort Stockton.

66. This study of the battle at Fort Lancaster is based on: William Frohock to John S. Loud, post adjutant, 27 December 1867, letters and telegrams received, Fort Stockton; post returns, Fort Stockton, December 1867, Southwest Collection; and Hatch to Morse, AAA general, District of Texas, 3 January 1868 (incorrectly stated as "1867"), letters and telegrams received, Fort Stockton. Quotes attributed to Frohock are from Frohock to Loud, 27 December 1867, and quotes attributed to Hatch are from Hatch to Morse, 3 January 1868. Information about the discovery of the slain soldiers is from Art Black, "The Forgotten Battle," *Texas Parks and Wildlife* 35, No. 6 (June 1977), 26.

67. Hatch to Morse, AAA general, District of Texas, 3 January and 20 February 1868, letters and telegrams sent, Fort Stockton.

68. First Lieutenant John S. Loud, post adjutant, to commanding officer, Company D, Ninth Cavalry, 28 March 1868, letters and telegrams sent, Fort Stockton; and Major James Franklin Wade to Captain C. E. Morse, AAA general, Fifth Military District, 16 June 1869, letters and telegrams sent, Fort Stockton.

69. Journal of Thomas B. Hunt, 29.

70. Loud to commanding officer, Company D, Ninth Cavalry, 28 March 1868.

71. Captain George Gamble to Brevet Captain C. S. Roberts, AAA general, Fifth Military District, 8 December 1868, letters and telegrams sent, Fort Stockton.

72. Loud to commanding officer, Company D, Ninth Cavalry, 28 March 1868.

73. Journal of Thomas B. Hunt, 29 (sketch of site).

74. R. Lauszky, surgeon, to E. D. Dimmick, post adjutant, 1 October 1868, letters and telegrams received, Fort Stockton.

75. Edward Hatch to Captain George Gamble, 1 July 1868, letters and telegrams received, Fort Stockton. Information on the distance is from the journal of Thomas B. Hunt, 28-29.

76. George Gamble to Brevet Captain C. S. Roberts, AAA general, Fifth Military District, 8 December 1868, letters and telegrams sent, Fort Stockton; and E. D. Judd, paymaster's officer, Fifth Military District, to Brevet Colonel H. Clay Wood, AA general, Fifth Military District, 11 November 1869, containing extracts from a letter of Major C. M. Tunnel, paymaster, Fort Concho, 21 October 1869, letters and telegrams received, Fort Stockton.

77. Wade to Morse, 16 June 1869.

78. Second Lieutenant G. Valois to AA general, Fifth Military District, 1 July 1869, letters and telegrams received, Fort Stockton.

79. "Journal of march of detachment, Company M, 9th Cavalry, commanded by Second Lieutenant Thomas C. Davenport, 9th U.S. Cavalry, from Fort Stockton, Texas to Independence Creek viz. old Fort Lancaster . . . pursuant to special order number 14, headquarters, Fort Stockton, Texas, Feb. 4, 1874," journal of marches, scouts, and expeditions, Fort Stockton.

80. Holmsley, interview with Haley.

81. Post returns, May 1871, Fort Stockton, Southwest Collection.

82. H. Clay Wood, AA general, to commanding officer, post of Fort Stockton, 27 April 1871, letters and telegrams received, Fort Stockton.

83. Post returns, Fort Stockton, January 1872, Southwest Collection.

84. W. R. Owen, interview with Haley, Carlsbad, New Mexico, 12 August 1926, typescript of interview, Haley Library.

85. Sam Woolford, ed., "The Burr G. Duval Diary," *SHQ* 65, No. 4 (April 1962), 496.

86. R. F. O'Beirne to AA general, Department of Texas, 11 September 1880, letters and telegrams sent, Fort Stockton.

87. Ripley, post adjutant, to Major E. D. Baker, quartermaster, San Antonio, 28 September 1880, letters and telegrams sent, Fort Stockton.

88. Hunter, *Trail Drivers*, 804-805.

89. Ibid., 116-117. The text gives the date of the drive as 1881, but internal evidence suggests that it is a misprint for 1891.

90. Ibid., 677.

91. Olin Smith, interviews, December 1992 and 2 August 1993.

92. Edna Brooks, taped telephone interview with author, Iraan, 4 August 1993.

93. Olin Smith, interview, 2 August 1993.

Chapter 8 • Other Crossings

1. For a discussion of Juan Cordona Lake, see Dearen, *Castle Gap*, 63-84.

2. This study of the Salt Trail is based on: Bolton, *Spanish Exploration*, 189-190, 325-330; Carlysle Graham Raht, *The Romance of Davis Mountains and Big Bend Country* (Odessa: Rahtbooks Company, Edition Texana, 1963), 31-33; Clayton Williams, *Never Again* Vol. 1: 18-20, Vol. 3: 4,5; Clayton Williams, *Last Frontier*, 117; O. W. Williams, *Mendosa*, 15-18; Victor J. Smith, "Early Spanish Exploration," 57-58; Marie Omo, taped interview with author, Crane, 3 May 1983; Billy Rankin, taped interview with author, Rankin, 17 May 1983; Haley, telephone interview with author, Midland, spring 1983; Haley, *Charles Goodnight*, 143 (based on a letter from Goodnight to Haley, 8 April 1927); I. C. "Tiny" Earp, taped interview with author, Crane County, 7 June 1983; and Alton Evans, taped interview with author, Crane, 3 May 1985.

3. I uncovered no mention of a ford at the site in my search of Fort Stockton headquarters records.

4. Julius Drew Henderson, "Memories of an Old Cowboy," 21, unpublished manuscript, Special Collections, Library, University of Texas of the Permian Basin, Odessa.

5. Ibid., 35.

6. Ibid., 70-71.

7. I. C. "Tiny" Earp reported that he once found a plaque on the bridge dated 1917. The plaque has since disappeared. Earp, taped telephone interview with author, Crane County, 17 October 1991.

8. Ibid. The other source is Clayton Williams, "Permian Basin History Buffs" (announcement of a Permian Historical Society field trip for 29 October 1977), Williams Collection, Haley Library.

9. Rankin, interview, 29 April 1991.

10. Newland, interview with Kelton.

11. U. S. Geological Survey, Girvin Southeast Quadrangle, 7.5-minute series (topographic map).

12. At least, not in any of the extensive records I searched.

13. W. R. Baggett, "Early Day Irrigation Ditches," 364-366. The quote attributed to Young is as paraphrased by Baggett. A second Adobe Walls lay well upstream near the present city of Pecos. Neither was associated with well-known Adobe Walls in the Texas Panhandle.

14. Second Lieutenant John Bigelow, Jr., to adjutant general, 9 December 1879, Fort Stockton.

15. Lieutenant W. H. Beck to post adjutant, 11 August 1878, Fort Stockton.

16. Second Lieutenant C. Esterly, map of a scout conducted 8-15 October 1878, Fort Stockton headquarters records, Fort Stockton.

17. Sam Woolford, ed., "The Burr G. Duval Diary," 497.

18. Newland, interview with Kelton.

19. McDonald, interview.

20. Rankin, interviews, 29 April 1991 and 28 November 1994. Although Rankin did not know the ford by name, his estimate of its distance above Spanish Dam—four miles—is within range of the actual travel distance of five and one-half miles. Measurement in "river miles" would yield a considerably greater distance.

21. Nora Locklin, composite of statements in telephone interviews with author, McCamey, 26 March 1992 and 21 July 1993.

22. As pinpointed by Paul Patterson, who crossed the ford several times in the 1920s. Patterson, taped interview with author, Pecos, 1 July 1993.

23. "Journal of march of detachment, Company M, 9th Cavalry, commanded by Second Lieutenant Thomas C. Davenport, 9th U.S. Cavalry, from Fort Stockton, Texas, to Independence Creek viz. old Fort Lancaster . . . pursuant to special order number 14, headquarters, Fort Stockton, Texas, February 4, 1874," Fort Stockton. The later "Army measurements" were by George W. Wedemeyer. See Clayton

Williams, ed., "Excerpts from the Diary of George W. Wedemeyer," *WTHA Year Book* 46 (1970), 161.

24. "Journal of march . . . commanded by First Lieutenant B. Dawson, 9th Cavalry, from Fort Stockton, Texas to Pecos River near Melvin Station in search of hostile Indians, pursuant to special order . . . dated headquarters, Fort Stockton, Texas, June 3, 1874," Fort Stockton.

25. Holmsley, interview with Haley. Pulliam's first name is as spelled in the *San Angelo Standard*, 29 May 1886, 3, col. 1. Halff's first name is as found in Ivan Murchison (as told to K. F. Neighbours), "Ranching on the Pecos at the Turn of the Twentieth Century," *WTHA Year Book* 53 (1977), 127. Alternate spellings of "Mayer" and "Meyer" are found in Clayton Williams, *Last Frontier*, 269.

26. Clayton Williams, "Diary of George W. Wedemeyer," 161-162.

27. Millard, *Cowpuncher*, 30. Although Millard refers to the site as Pontoon Crossing, the fact that he swam his horse rather than crossed by bridge suggests he actually forded S Crossing.

28. J. Frank Dobie, *The Longhorns* (New York: Bramhall House, 1941), 184.

29. Holmsley, interview with Haley.

30. Nix, interview with Patterson.

31. Patterson, interview, 1 July 1993.

32. For Narbo's, see "Pecos County 28 Years Ago," *The Fort Stockton Pioneer*, 17 September 1908; Charles Goodnight, interview with Haley, Clarendon, 12 September 1928, Haley Library; Jones, interview with Haley; W. R. Owen, interview with Haley, 2 March 1933; Jim K. Millwee, interviews with Haley, Lubbock, 3 July 1932 and 13 September 1932, Haley Library; Fort Stockton headquarters to adjutant general, 9 December 1879, letters and telegrams sent, Fort Stockton; "Journal of detachment of Company M, Ninth Cavalry, commanded by Lieutenant Thomas C. Davenport, Ninth Cavalry,

on escort duty with cattle to Narboe's Crossing, Pecos River, pursuant to special order . . . headquarters, Fort Stockton, August 12, 1874," and accompanying map; and Second Lieutenant John Bigelow to adjutant general, 9 December 1879, journal of marches, scouts, and expeditions, Fort Stockton. For Pecos Falls, see T. U. Taylor, "Pioneer Points on the Pecos," *Frontier Times* 17, No. 11, (August 1940), 435-436; and Bigelow to adjutant general, 9 December 1879. For Frazier's, see "Journal of scout of detachment, Company M, 9th Cavalry, commanded by Second Lieutenant Thomas Davenport, Ninth Cavalry, from Fort Stockton, Texas, to Pecos Falls, via Horsehead Crossing, returning via Frazier Crossing and Monument Springs, pursuant to special order . . . dated March 16, 1874," and accompanying map, journal of marches, scouts, and expeditions, Fort Stockton; and journal of Davenport on escort to Marboe's Crossing and accompanying map. For Hackberry, see Bigelow to adjutant general, 9 December 1879. For Mosely, see Rankin, interviews, 29 April 1991 and 28 November 1994; Cora Dawson Smith, interview; and Enoch Smith, telephone interview with author, McCamey, 13 July 1993. Rankin, whose lease ranch once included Mosely Crossing, estimated it to be four travel miles downstream from Horsehead. For Sixmile and Fourmile, see Bud Mayes, taped interview with author, Ozona, 22 February 1990, and videotaped interview with author, Ozona, 30 April 1991.

Epilogue

1. Crawford, "A History of West Texas," 60.

2. Nora Gentry Locklin, *Sixty Three Years of Married Life on the West Texas Plains* (unpublished manuscript, 1988), 49-50, excerpt in author's possesion.

3. Bliss, "Reminiscences," Vol. 1, 189. Bliss first crossed the Pecos in October 1855. For more about the water's quality in frontier times, see Dearen, *Castle Gap*, 42-43.

4. "'World's Worst' is Pecos Water," *Pecos Enterprise*, 15 April 1932, Permian Basin Petroleum Museum, Library, and Hall of Fame, Midland.

5. Ross, "Historic Crossing Submerged."

6. Newland, interview with Kelton.

7. Shafer, *Ancient Texans*, 49.

Interviews by Author
Boren, Walter, Post, Texas, 8 August 1990.
Brooks, Edna, Iraan, Texas, 4 August 1993.
Earp, I. C., Crane County, Texas, 7 June 1983, 17 October 1991.
Eddins, L. B. "Bill," Kermit, Texas, 5 September 1989.
Eisenwine, Norman, Pecos, Texas, 1 July 1993.
Evans, Alton, Crane, Texas, 3 May 1985.
Glass, David, Sterling County, Texas, 13 March 1992.
Haley, J. Evetts, Midland, Texas, spring 1983, 7 October 1992, 4
    November 1993.
Hinton, Harwood, Austin, Texas, summer 1993.
Hubbs, Barney, Pecos, Texas, 19 March 1992.
Locklin, Nora, McCamey, Texas, 26 March 1992, 21 July 1993.
Mayes, Bud, Ozona, Texas, 22 February 1990, 30 April 1991.
McDonald, Roy, Pecos County, Texas, 12 August 1982.
McFadden, Leslie, Rankin, Texas, 21 August 1995.
Midkiff, Tyson, Rankin, Texas, 9 August 1989, 11 December 1990,
    29 April 1991.
Omo, Marie, Crane, Texas, 3 May 1983.
Patterson, Paul, Crane, Texas, 29 April 1991, 1 July 1993.
Rankin, Billy, Rankin, Texas, 17 May 1983, 9 August 1989, 29
    April 1991, 28 November 1994.

Reding, Gid, Fort Stockton, Texas, 1 September 1989.
Smith, Cora Dawson, Iraan, Texas, 12 August 1982.
Smith, Olin, Pecos County, Texas, December 1992; Pecos County
      and Terrell County, Texas, 2 August 1993.
Smith, Enoch, McCamey, Texas, 13 July 1993.
Stillwell, Hallie, Brewster County, Texas, 10 July 1993.
Vandevanter, Tom, Rankin, Texas, 19 March 1993.
Villalba, Chon, Fort Stockton, Texas, 9 February 1990.
Wendorf, Fred, Dallas, Texas, fall 1982, 10 June 1991.
Wilson, William B., Midland, Texas, 28 November 1994.
Witt, Jim, Loving, New Mexico, 17 July 1993.

**Taped Interviews, Southwest Collection, Texas Tech University,
Lubbock, Texas**
Dyer, Russell, Sanderson, Texas, summer 1968 (by Paul Patterson).
McElroy, Erving, Lubbock, Texas, 1 June 1972 (by David Murrah).
Nix, Mrs. Will (Opal), Rankin, Texas, 30 May 1968 (by Paul
      Patterson).
Slack, Clay, Pecos, Texas, 5 July 1968 (by Paul Patterson).
Ussery, Huling, Carlsbad, New Mexico, 22 February 1982 (by
      Richard Mason).

**Interview Transcripts, Nita Stewart Haley Memorial Library,
Midland, Texas**
Arnett, D. N., Colorado City, Texas, 18 October 1926 (by J. Evetts
      Haley).
Ballard, Charles, Luna, New Mexico, 9 June 1939 (by J. Evetts
      Haley and Hervey Chesley).
Beal, H. D., Gail, Texas, 11 September 1931 (by J. Evetts Haley).
Bell, Irbin H., El Paso, Texas, 18 March 1927 (by J. Evetts Haley).
Calohan, Lod, Kansas City, Missouri, 1 January 1926 (by J. Evetts
      Haley).
Casey, Robert Adam, Pichacho, New Mexico, 25 June 1937 (by J.
      Evetts Haley)

Coe, George, Glencoe, New Mexico, 20 March 1927 (by J. Evetts Haley).

Goodnight, Charles, Clarendon, Texas, 12 September 1928 (by J. Evetts Haley).

Holmsley, W. H., Midland, 17 October 1926 (by J. Evetts Haley).

Jones, James P., Rocky Arroyo, New Mexico, 13-14 January 1927 (by J. Evetts Haley).

McNairy, D. H., Mineral Wells, Texas, 22 January 1932 (by J. Evetts Haley).

Millwee, Jim K., Lubbock, Texas, 3 July 1932 and 13 September 1932 (by J. Evetts Haley).

Mullens, James W., Roswell, New Mexico, 14 January 1927 (by J. Evetts Haley).

Owens, George, Pecos, Texas, 10 January 1927 (by J. Evetts Haley).

Owen, W. R., Carlsbad, New Mexico, 12 August 1926, 2 March 1933 and 24 June 1937 (by J. Evetts Haley).

Roberson, G. W., Vega, Texas, 30 June 1926 (by J. Evetts Haley).

White, C. J., Sheridan, Wyoming, 22 April 1928 (by J. Evetts Haley).

Wier, W., Monument, New Mexico, 22 June 1937 (by J. Evetts Haley).

Windham, A. T., Pecos, Texas, 10 January 1927 (by J. Evetts Haley).

Miscellaneous Taped Interviews in Author's Possession

Bartholomew, Ed, Fort Davis, Texas, October 1991 (by Mike Cox).

Hubbs, Barney, Pecos, Texas, 21 October 1991 (by Mike Cox).

Leftwich, Bill, Fort Davis, Texas, fall 1991 (by Mike Cox).

Newland, Cliff, Upton County, Texas, 23 August 1964 (by Elmer Kelton).

Military Records

Fort Lancaster, Texas. Post returns, 1855-1861. National Archives, Washington, D.C.

Fort Stockton, Texas. Post returns, 1859-1861, 1867-1886.
(National Archives microfilm) Southwest Collection, Texas Tech
     University, Lubbock, Texas, and Fort Stockton Public Library,
     Fort Stockton, Texas. Unless otherwise indicated, records
     referred to in notes are on microfilm at the Fort Stockton
     Public Library.
————————. Letters and telegrams sent, letters and telegrams
     received, journal of marches, scouts, and expeditions, 1867-
     1886. (National Archives microfilm) Fort Stockton Public
     Library, Fort Stockton.
U.S. Department of War, Civil Works Map File, Q-154, Record
     Group 77, National Archives, Washington, D.C.
————————. Records of the Adjutant General's Office, Record
     Group 94, National Archives, Washington, D.C.
U.S. Army Commands, Record Group 98, National Archives,
     Washington, D.C.

Maps
(U. S. Geological Survey, 7.5-minute series, topographic, unless
otherwise indicated)

Girvin Southeast Quadrangle, Texas.
Indian Mesa Quadrangle, Texas.
Ligon Ranch Quadrangle, Texas.
McCamey South Quadrangle, Texas.
"Map of Texas and Part of New Mexico, compiled in the Bureau of
     Topographical Engineers, chiefly for military purposes, 1857."
     Austin: Ranger Canyon Press, n. d.
Red Bluff Quadrangle, (Eddy County) New Mexico.
Red Bluff Quadrangle, Texas.
Table Top Mountain Quadrangle, Texas.

Books
Adams, Ramon F. *Western Words: A Dictionary of the American*
     West. Norman: University of Oklahoma Press, rev. edition, 1968.

Armes, George A. *Ups and Downs of an Army Officer*. Washington: publisher not known, 1900.

Bieber, Ralph P., ed. *Exploring Southwestern Trails 1846-1854*. Glendale: Arthur H. Clark Company, 1938.

Bolton, Herbert Eugene. *Spanish Exploration in the Southwest*. New York: Barnes and Noble, Inc., reprint, 1952.

Cline, Donald. *Alias Billy the Kid: The Man Behind the Legend*. Santa Fe: Sunstone Press, 1986.

Conkling, Roscoe P., and Conkling, Margaret B. *The Butterfield Overland Mail, 1857-1869, Vol. 1*. Glendale: Arthur H. Clark Company, 1947.

Dearen, Patrick. *Portraits of the Pecos Frontier*. Lubbock: Texas Tech University Press, 1993.

——————. *Castle Gap and the Pecos Frontier*. Fort Worth: Texas Christian University Press, 1988.

Dobie, J. Frank. *A Vaquero of the Brush Country*. New York: Grosset and Dunlap Publishers, reprint, n. d., originally published by Southwest Press, 1929.

——————. *The Longhorns*. New York: Bramhall House, 1941.

Egan, Ferol. *The El Dorado Trail: The Story of the Gold Rush Routes Across Mexico*. New York: McGraw-Hill Book Company, 1970.

Fiftieth Anniversary West of the Pecos Rodeo, 50-Year History Edition, 1979.

Ford, John Salmon. *Rip Ford's Texas*. Austin: University of Texas Press, 1963.

Frazer, Robert W., ed. *Mansfield on the Condition of the Western Forts 1853-54*. Norman: University of Oklahoma Press, 1963.

Gillett, James B. *Six Years with the Texas Rangers, 1875 to 1881*. New Haven: Yale University Press, 1925.

Haley, J. Evetts. *Charles Goodnight: Cowman and Plainsman*. Norman: University of Oklahoma Press, 10th printing, 1987.

——————, ed. *The Diary of Michael Erskine*. Midland: Nita Stewart Haley Memorial Library, 1979.

——————. *Fort Concho and the Texas Frontier*. San Angelo:

San Angelo Standard-Times, 1952.

————. *Rough Times—Tough Fiber*. Canyon: Palo Duro Press, 1976.

Heartsill, W. W. *Fourteen Hundred and 91 Days in the Confederate Army: A Journal Kept by W. W. Heartsill for Four Years, One Month and One Day*. Jackson, Tenn.: McCowat-Mercer Press, facsimile edition of original 1876 edition, 1953.

Hinkle, James F. *Early Days of a Cowboy on the Pecos*. Santa Fe: Stagecoach Press, reprint, 1965. Originally published, 1937.

A History of Crockett County. San Angelo: Crockett County Historical Society American Revolution Bicentennial Project, Anchor Publishing Company, 1976.

Holmes, Kenneth L., ed. and compiler. *Covered Wagon Women: Diaries and Letters from the Western Trails 1840-1890, Vol. 1 1840-1849*. Glendale: Arthur H. Clark Company, 1983.

————. *Covered Wagon Women: Diaries and Letters from the Western Trails 1840-1890, Vol. 9 1864-1868*. Spokane: Arthur H. Clark Company, 1990.

Hughes, Alton. *Pecos: A History of the Pioneer West*. Seagraves, Texas: Pioneer Book Publishers, 1978.

Hunter, J. Marvin, ed. and compiler, *The Trail Drivers of Texas*. Austin: University of Texas Press, reprint, 1985.

Klasner, Lily. *My Girlhood Among Outlaws*. Tucson: University of Arizona Press, 1972.

Lands of Texas. Approved by the Texas State Legislature 10 March 1875.

Lesley, Lewis Burt, ed. *Uncle Sam's Camels: The Journal of May Humphreys Stacey*. Cambridge: Harvard University Press, 1929.

Marcy, Randolph B. *The Prairie Traveler: A Handbook for Overland Expeditions*. Williamstown, Mass.: Corner House Publishers, facsimile reprint, 1968. Originally published New York: Harper, 1859.

McConnell, Joseph Carroll. *The West Texas Frontier Vol. II*. Jacksboro, Texas: publisher not known, 1933-1939.

Millard, F. S. A *Cowpuncher of the Pecos*. J. Marvin Hunter, n.d.

Myres, Sandra L., ed. *Ho for California! Women's Overland Diaries from the Huntington Library*. San Marino: Huntington Library, 1980.

Nash, Jay Robert. *Encyclopedia of Western Lawmen and Outlaws*. New York: Paragon House, 1992.

Newcomb, W. W., Jr. *The Indians of Texas*. Austin: University of Texas Press, 1961.

O'Neal, Bill. *Encyclopedia of Western Gunfighters*. Norman: University of Oklahoma Press, 1979.

Ormsby, Waterman L. *The Butterfield Overland Mail*. San Marino: Huntington Library, 1955.

Parsons, Chuck. *Clay Allison, Portrait of a Shootist*. Seagraves, Texas: Pioneer Book Publishers, 1983.

Powers, Stephen. *Afoot and Alone: A Walk from Sea to Sea by the Southern Route*. Hartford, Conn.: Columbian Book Company, 1886.

Raht, Carlysle Graham. *The Romance of Davis Mountains and Big Bend Country*. Odessa: Rahtbooks Company, Edition Texana, 1963.

Reid, John C. *Reid's Tramp, or a Journal of the Incidents of Ten Months Travel Through Texas, New Mexico, Arizona, Sonora, and California*. Austin: Steck Company, reprint, 1935. Originally published 1858.

Reports of Explorations and Surveys to Ascertain the Most Practicable and Economical Route for a Railroad from the Mississippi River to the Pacific Ocean, Vol. II, 33rd Cong., 2nd sess., House of Representatives Executive Document No. 91. Washington: 1855.

Reports of the Secretary of War with Reconnaissance of Routes from San Antonio to El Paso, 31st Cong., 1st sess., Senate Executive Document No. 64. Washington: 1850.

Richardson, Albert D. *Beyond the Mississippi*. Hartford, Conn.: American Publishing Company, 1867.

Santleben, August. *A Texas Pioneer*. New York and Washington: Neal Publishing Company, 1910.

Scobee, Barry. *Old Fort Davis*. San Antonio: Naylor Company, 1947.

Shafer, Harry J. *Ancient Texans: Rock Art and Lifeways Along the Lower Pecos*. Houston: Gulf Publishing Company for Witte Museum of the San Antonio Museum Association, 1986.

Syers, William Edward. *Off the Beaten Trail*. Waco: Texian Press, 1971.

The Texas Almanac for 1859. Galveston: The Galveston News.

The Texas Almanac for 1867. Galveston: The Galveston News.

The Texas Almanac for 1870. Galveston: The Galveston News.

Texas Almanac 1970-71. Dallas: A. H. Belo Corporation, 1969.

1990-91 Texas Almanac. Dallas: The Dallas Morning News, 1989.

Turpin, Solveig A., (text) and Zintgraff, Jim, (photography). *Pecos River Rock Art*. San Antonio: Sandy McPherson Publishing Company, 1991.

Utley, Robert M. *Billy the Kid: A Short and Violent Life*. Lincoln: University of Nebraska Press, 1989.

Wallace, Ernest, and Hoebel, E. Adamson. *The Comanches: Lords of the South Plains*. Norman: University of Oklahoma Press, 1986. Originally published, 1952.

The War of the Rebellion: A Compilation of the Official Records of the Union and Confederate Armies, series 1, 1. Washington: Government Printing Office, 1880-1901, reprint edition by National Historical Society, Gettysburg, 1972.

Williams, Clayton. *Never Again*, 3 vols. San Antonio: Naylor Company, 1969.

—————. *Texas' Last Frontier: Fort Stockton and the Trans-Pecos, 1861-1895*. College Station: Texas A&M University Press, 1982.

Williams, J. W. *Old Texas Trails*. Burnet: Eakin Press, 1979.

Williams, O. W. *Mendosa—1684, in Pecos County*. Fort Stockton: 1902.

—————. *Pioneer Surveyor-Frontier Lawyer: The Personal Narrative of O. W. Williams, 1877-1902*. S. D. Myres, ed. El Paso: Texas Western College Press, 1966.

Williams, R. H. *With the Border Ruffians: Memories of the Far West, 1852-1868*. E. W. Williams, ed. London: John Murray, 1908.

Wilson, John P. *Fort Sumner, New Mexico*. Santa Fe: Museum of New Mexico, 1974.

Journals and Magazines

Austerman, Wayne R. "Giddings' Station, A Forgotten Landmark on the Pecos." *The Permian Historical Annual* 21 (1981): 3-12.

Baggett, W. R. "Early Day Irrigation Ditches on the Pecos." *Frontier Times* 19, No. 10 (July 1942): 364-366.

Bender, A. B. "Opening Routes Across West Texas, 1848-1850." *Southwestern Historical Quarterly* 37, No. 2 (October 1933): 116-135.

Black, Art. "The Forgotten Battle." *Texas Parks and Wildlife* 35, No. 6 (June 1977): 25-26.

Bowles, J. Frank. "Overland Trip to California in 1850." *Frontier Times* 4, No. 5 (February 1927): 12-16.

Call, Oscar. "Diary of Oscar Call, July 8-August 4, 1858." *Stalkin' Kin* 2, No. 4 (May 1975): 167-170.

Cochran, W. C. "A Long Cattle Drive to Montana." *Frontier Times* 22, No. 9 (June 1945): 253-256.

—————. "Walter C. Cochran's Memoirs of Early Day Cattlemen." Betty Orbeck, ed. *The Texas Permian Historical Annual* 1, No. 1 (August 1961): 36-42.

Cross, Cora Melton. "Breaking a Stampede of 10,000 Buffalo." *Frontier Times* 6, No. 7 (April 1929): 273-277.

Curless, William. "Passage of McCulloch's Emigrant Train Across the Staked Plains." *West Texas Historical Association Year Book* 30 (October 1954): 141-154.

Dearen, Patrick. "Horsehead to Castle Gap: Trailing the Past." *True West* 39, No. 8 (August 1992): 22-27.

Duke, Escal F., ed. "A Description of the Route from San Antonio to El Paso by Captain Edward S. Meyer." *West Texas Historical Association Year Book* 49 (1973): 128-141.

Eads, Rachel. "A Trying Trip Across the Desert." *Frontier Times* 22,

No. 9 (June 1945): 243-246.

Fowler, Brad C. Letter of 15 August 1853 in "Wagon Trains and Cattle Herds on the Trail in the 1850's." *West Texas Historical Association Year Book* 30 (October 1954): 141-154.

Grant, Ben O., and Webb, J. R. "On the Cattle Trail and Buffalo Range, Joe S. McCombs." *West Texas Historical Association Year Book* 2 (November 1935): 93-101.

Haley, J. Evetts, ed. "A Log of the Texas-California Cattle Trail, 1854." *Southwestern Historical Quarterly* 35, No. 3 (January 1932): 208-237.

Hunter, J. Marvin. "Midnight Battle at Fort Lancaster." *Frontier Times* 21, No. 9 (June 1944): 366-370.

Kenner, Charles. "The Origins of the 'Goodnight' Trail Reconsidered." *Southwestern Historical Quarterly* 77, No. 3 (January 1974): 390-394.

King, Grace Thormann. "Captain John Pope, First Driller in the Permian Basin." *The Texas Permian Historical Annual* 2, No. 1 (August 1962): 11-23.

Lammons, Frank Bishop. "Operation Camel: An Experiment in Animal Transportation in Texas, 1857-1860." *Southwestern Historical Quarterly* 61, No. 1 (July 1957): 20-50.

Mahon, Emmie Giddings W., and Kielman, Chester V. "Giddings and the San Antonio-San Diego Mail Line." *Southwestern Historical Quarterly* 61, No. 2 (October 1957): 220-239.

Mansfield, J. K. "Colonel J. K. F. Mansfield's Report of the Inspection of the Department of Texas in 1856." *Southwestern Historical Quarterly* 42, No. 2 (October 1938): 122-148.

——————. "Colonel J. K. F. Mansfield's Report of the Inspection of the Department of Texas in 1856." *Southwestern Historical Quarterly* 42, No. 3 (January 1939): 215-257.

Martin, Mabelle Eppard. "California Emigrant Roads through Texas." *Southwestern Historical Quarterly* 28, No. 4 (April 1925): 287-301.

——————, ed. "From Texas to California in 1849: Lewis B. Harris to a Brother." *Southwestern Historical Quarterly* 29, No. 3 (January

1926): 215-220.

Murchison, Ivan. As told to K. F. Neighbours. "Ranching on the Pecos at the Turn of the Twentieth Century." *West Texas Historical Association Year Book* 53 (1977): 127-136.

Myers, Lee. "Pope's Wells." *New Mexico Historical Review* 38, No. 4 (October 1963): 273-299.

Myres, Sandra L., ed. "A Woman's View of the Texas Frontier, 1874: The Diary of Emily K. Andrews." *Southwestern Historical Quarterly* 86, No. 1 (July 1982): 49-80.

Patterson, Paul. "A Forgotten Empire of the Pecos." *The Cattleman* (May 1943): 24-25.

Posey, Cora Addison. "Another Trail Driver: William Hinton Posey," *Frontier Times* 8, No. 5 (February 1931): 215-219.

Ramsey, Grover C. "Camp Melvin, Crockett County, Texas." *West Texas Historical Association Year Book* 37 (October 1961): 137-146.

Rasch, Philip J. "The Story of Jessie J. Evans." *Panhandle-Plains Historical Review* 33 (1960): 108-121.

"Record of Engagement with Hostile Indians in Texas, 1868-1882." *West Texas Historical Association Year Book* 9 (October 1933): 101-118.

Scannell, Jack C. "Henry Skillman, Texas Frontiersman." *The Permian Historical Annual* 18 (December 1978): 19-31.

Smith, Victor J. "Early Spanish Exploration in the Big Bend of Texas." *West Texas Historical and Scientific Society*, No. 2 (1928): 55-68.

Syers, Ed. "Map Keeps Secret Well, But Treasure Hunters Hard to Discourage." *Western Chronicles* 3, No. 1, Fort Stockton: Pecos County Historical Commission, fall 1981): 2.

Taylor, T. U. "Pioneer Points on the Pecos." *Frontier Times* 17, No. 11 (August 1940): 435-438.

White, Grace Miller. "Oliver Loving, the First Trail Driver." *Frontier Times* 19, No. 7 (April 1942): 269-276.

Williams, Clayton. "The First Two Irrigation Projects on the Pecos River in Texas." *The Permian Historical Annual* 15 (December

1975): 2-6.

──────. "The Pontoon Bridge on the Pecos, 1869-1886." *The Permian Historical Annual* 18 (December 1978): 3-17.

──────. "That Topographical Ghost—Horsehead Crossing!" *The Permian Basin Historical Annual* 17 (December 1977): 37-56.

──────, ed. "Excerpts from the Diary of George W. Wedemeyer." *West Texas Historical Association Year Book* 46 (1970): 156-166.

Woolford, Sam, ed. "The Burr G. Duval Diary." *Southwestern Historical Quarterly* 65, No. 4 (April 1962): 487-511.

Newspapers

"Legendary Pecos crossing located," *Austin American-Statesman,* 20 March 1995.

Austin Democratic Statesman, 17, 18 October 1876.

The Colorado Tribune (Matagorda, Texas), 21 July 1854.

Dallas Herald, 7 August 1858.

The Eddy Argus (Eddy, New Mexico), 30 April 1892.

El Paso Daily Times, 15 May 1897.

The Fort Stockton Pioneer, 10 September 1908, 17 September 1908.

Fort Worth Gazette, 16 January 1885.

Galveston Daily News, 28 June 1878.

Galveston Journal, 26 May 1854.

Globe Livestock Journal (Dodge City, Kansas), 27 April 1886, 25 May 1886.

Herald (San Antonio), 18 April 1868, 10 November 1868.

Pecos Enterprise, 15 April 1932, 27 July 1934, 31 July 1936.

Rocky Mountain News (Denver, Colorado), 29 January 1886.

San Angelo Standard, 13 September 1884, 21 February 1885, 29 May 1886.

San Antonio Express, 13 October 1876, 19 October 1876, 3 November 1876, 4 May 1877, 18 May 1877, 25 May 1877, 14 August 1877, 17 August 1877, 22 August 1877, 30 August 1877, 28 October 1877, 31 October 1877, 23 December 1877, 13 January 1883 (sometimes styled *San Antonio Daily*

Express).

Standard (Clarksville, Texas), 1 October 1853, 20 July 1861.

Sterling City (Texas) *News-Record*, 24 April 1936, 11 December 1942, 17 December 1943.

Texas Live Stock Journal (Fort Worth, Texas), 5 December 1885, 29 May 1886.

Waco Register, 21 April 1866.

The Washington Union (Washington City), 12 October 1858.

Letters and Manuscripts

Bliss, Zenas R. "Reminiscences." (5 volumes, Nita Stewart Haley Memorial Library, Midland, Texas).

Caruthers, L. B., to John B. Jones, 14 June 1880 (transcript, Nita Stewart Haley Memorial Library, Midland).

Caruthers, L. B., to C. L. Nevill, 8 June 1880, 14 June 1880 (transcripts, Nita Stewart Haley Memorial Library, Midland).

Dean, John M., county attorney, Presidio County, to O. M. Roberts, governor of Texas, 21 May 1880 (transcript, Nita Stewart Haley Memorial Library, Midland).

Gage, R. D., to Maurice G. Fulton, 30 January 1929 (Nita Stewart Haley Memorial Library, Midland).

Glass, J. L. Journal (in the possession of David Glass and family, Sterling County, Texas).

Goodnight, Charles. "Recollections II" (Nita Stewart Haley Memorial Library, Midland).

Grigsby, Melburn Glass. With quotations from J. L. G. notebook added by Dan Glass. "The Glass Family: A Souvenir History and Genealogy 1883-1983" (in the possession of David Glass and family, Sterling County, Texas).

—————, compiler, and Willene Glass Boger. "The Life of James Jefferson Lafayette Glass, 1861-1947," 1967 (in the possession of David Glass and family, Sterling County, Texas).

Hayter, Delmar. "The Crookedest River in the World: A Social and Economic Development of the Pecos River Valley from 1878 to 1950." (dissertation, Texas Tech University, Lubbock,

Texas).

Henderson, Julius Drew. "Memories of an Old Cowboy." (Special Collections, Library, University of Texas of the Permian Basin, Odessa, Texas).

Hubbs, Barney. "Indian Burial Grounds, Immigrant Crossing on the Pecos, Rancher Discovers Skeletons." (cutlines on photo display, West of the Pecos Museum, Pecos, Texas).

Johnson, J. L., Sr., to Miguel A. Otero, 21 March 1929. (transcript, Nita Stewart Haley Memorial Library, Midland).

Locklin, Nora Gentry. "Sixty Three Years of Married Life on the West Texas Plains," 1988 (excerpt in author's possession).

Loving, Oliver, to R. M. Garden, Weatherford, Texas, 22 May 1866. (Nita Stewart Haley Memorial Library, Midland).

Nevill, C. L., to John B. Jones, 5 September 1880. (transcript, Nita Stewart Haley Memorial Library, Midland).

Oden, B. A. "Early Cowboy Days in New Mexico and Texas." (typescript, Nita Stewart Haley Memorial Library, Midland).

"Outrages and Indian Raids in Presidio County from June 1, 1879 to June 1, 1880." (transcripts from the office of the adjutant general of Texas, Nita Stewart Haley Memorial Library, Midland).

Rettlesen and Deljehan, S. and W. Schulz, Ynocente Ochoa, B. Schuster and Company, to Adjutant General J. B. Jones, 21 May 1880 (transcript, Nita Stewart Haley Memorial Library, Midland).

Strentzel, John Theophil. "Biography of John Theophil Strentzel." (Nita Stewart Haley Memorial Library, Midland).

Williams, Clayton. "F. W. Young came to Fort Stockton," handwritten notes (Nita Stewart Haley Memorial Library, Midland).

—————. "Permian Basin History Buffs." Announcement of a Permian Historical Society field trip for 29 October 1977. (Clayton Williams Papers, Nita Stewart Haley Memorial Library, Midland).

Collections

Fort Lancaster (Texas) State Historical Park Archives.

J. Evetts Haley Collection, Nita Stewart Haley Memorial Library, Midland, Texas.

Map Collection, Nita Stewart Haley Memorial Library, Midland.

Clayton Wheat Williams Collection, Nita Stewart Haley Memorial Library, Midland.

Special Collections, Library, University of Texas of the Permian Basin, Odessa, Texas.

Documentary Film

Dearen, Patrick, and Ely, Glen Sample. With contributions by Cox, Mike. *Graveyard of the West: The Pecos River of Texas Where Myth Meets History*. Austin: Forest Glen TV Productions, Inc., 1993.